Lukács' Concept of Dialectic

GW00457032

Lukács' Concept of Dialectic

with Biography, Bibliography and Documents

István Mészáros

AAKAR

LUKÁCS' CONCEPT OF DIALECTIC
István Mészáros

© István Mészáros 1972
© Aakar Books for South Asia 2013

First Published in India 2013
Reprint 2017

ISBN 978-93-5002-215-3

Published by
AAKAR BOOKS
28 E Pocket IV, Mayur Vihar Phase I, Delhi 110 091
Phones: 011 2279 5505, 011 2279 5641
aakarbooks@gmail.com

Printed at
Sapra Brothers, Delhi 110 092

CONTENTS

PREFACE

Shortly after completing his *Aesthetics*, Lukács set
out to realize a long-standing plan : to write a systematic *Ethics* which should have been the final sum-
mation of his life's work. He produced an outline
without difficulty and in a letter from Budapest, dated
10 May 1962, he indicated the general approach of
this work, rendered explicit also in its projected title :
*Die Stelle der Ethik im System menschlichen Aktivi-
täten* (The Place of Ethics in the System of Human
Activities). Twenty months later, however, he was
complaining that his *Ethics* was proceeding "very
slowly. It has proved necessary for me to write first a
big introductory part on the ontology of social being,
and the latter, too, proceeds very slowly." (Budapest,
13 January 1964.)

The "introductory part" turned out to be a massive
work of nearly 2000 pages which bears the title of

The Ontology of Social Being. Furthermore, the latter
in turn made necessary for Lukács the writing of his
Prolegomena to the Ontology of Social Being—a work
to which he was trying to put the finishing touches
when he died on the 4th of June 1971. Thus, he
could not realize the plan that has been perhaps the
nearest to his heart: the elaboration of the fundamental principles of a Marxist ethics. Nevertheless,
it must be remembered in all future discussion of
Lukács' *Ontology of Social Being* that it was conceived as an integral part of his quest for identifying
the proper ethical framework of socialist human
relations.

Naturally, a comprehensive intellectual biography
of Lukács is unthinkable without a close study of his
Ontology and *Prolegomena*. Equally, the analysis of
a great deal of other material left by Lukács—including a major aesthetic work from his youth, discovered
among his manuscripts after his death—must be an
organic part of a full-scale biography. Thus, inevitably, my original project is bound to take years to
complete. In the meantime, in response to student
demand, I have decided to publish in this volume
my essay on *Lukács' Concept of Dialectic.* I hope
that this essay which deals, however concisely, with
Lukács' work as a whole in terms of its centrally
important concepts, on the basis of his published
writings as well as of some hitherto unpublished
material, can facilitate the study of Lukács' many-

7

sided and highly complex work. Also, to make study easier, I have included in this volume extensive biographical data and a comprehensive bibliography.

I wish to express my thanks to Lukács' sister, Mrs Maria Popper, for the opportunity of clarifying conversations and for the material she has put at my disposal.

Sussex University,   I.M.
Brighton, January 1972

LUKÁCS' CONCEPT
OF DIALECTIC

*"Der Zwiespalt von Sein und Sollen ist nicht aufge-
hoben"—Die Theorie des Romans.*
(The division between "is" and "ought" is not
transcended—*The Theory of the Novel*)

1. Issue

1. Introductory

The problems of dialectic occupy a central place
in Lukács' thought. Two of his greatest philosophical
works make this clear even on the title page:
Geschichte und Klassenbewusstsein (History and
Class Consciousness) bears the subtitle *Studien über
marxistische Dialektik*, and *Der Junge Hegel* (The
Young Hegel) is subtitled *Über die Beziehungen von
Dialektik und Ökonomie* (On the Relations between
Dialectic and Economics). Similarly, one of his major
philosophical essays is entitled: *Moses Hess und die
Probleme der idealistischen Dialektik* (Moses Hess and
the Problems of Idealistic Dialectic). But Lukács' con-
cern for the problems of dialectics goes well beyond
these works, important though they are on their own.
Thus his work *Über die Besonderheit als Kategorie der
Ästhetik* (On the "Specific" as a Category of Aesthetics) investigates, in its broadest connections, a central

category of dialectics; *Die Zerstörung der Vernunft*
(The Destruction of Reason) systematically explores
the contrasts between "irrationalism"—in its most
developed, German version—and "dialectical rationality", insisting on the validity of the latter as opposed
to all forms of "irrationalistic mystification"; *Die
Eigenart des Ästhetischen* (The Particularity of the
Aesthetical Element), Lukács' massive *Aesthetic*, contains several chapters in which the discussion of some
central issues of a materialistic dialectic predomin-
ates; and his last great systematic work, *Zur Ontologie
des gesellschaftlichen Seins* (Towards an Ontology of
Social Being), on the evidence of his own accounts of
it, is centred around the problems of dialectics. (In
fact the latter is the first attempt at producing a
systematic Marxist dialectical Ontology.) But fully
to comprehend the extraordinary wealth of his ideas
on dialectics in all its details one should also take into
account, in addition to the major systematic works,
the innumerable references to the manifold aspects of
dialectics contained in his essays and articles on
History, Politics, Economics, History of Philosophy,
History of Aesthetics, History of Literature, Epistemology, Aesthetics, Ethics, Sociology, Party matters,
Cultural Policy, Ideology, etc.

The main reasons behind his constant preoccupa-
tion with the problems of dialectics could be briefly
characterized as follows:

(i) The prevalence of "vulgar Marxism" in the

organized working-class movement; dogmatic attacks on dialectics and glorifications of pedestrian, mechanistic materialism in a variety of its versions; ideological and political-organizational trends expressing the same mechanistic dogmatism. (Lukács' rigorous defence of Hegel must be understood in this connection : as a defence of the universal methodological validity of the dialectical approach.)

(ii) Problems of dialectics are assigned a central place in Marx's "intellectual Testament"—the tasks he formulated in the field of theory but could never realize himself : that is, the systematic elaboration of the principles of Marxism in History, Logic, Aesthetics, Ontology, Epistemology, Ethics, etc. (E.g. the issue of paramount importance—the relationship between "system" and "history"—is a problem of dialectic *par excellence*.) Lukács, perceiving his tasks in this respect, had to return time and again to the problems of dialectics.

(iii) The problematic character of dialectic and of "dialectical rationality" in an age in which mankind is repeatedly menaced with self-destruction. The Hegelian "ruse of Reason" (*List der Vernunft*) as the objective dialectical law of historical development, and its Marxian version as "ruse of history", seem to be inevitably problematical at a time when human history is in danger of "outwitting itself", darkening thus the perspectives of numerous philosophical and artistic trends. Lukács' unceasing reassertion of the

13

validity of dialectic is to be considered against this background, even if his answers often over-emphasize one side of this complex of problems, radically condemning all kinds of "irrationality" and "decadentism". Thus, to give a detailed account of his ideas on the various aspects of dialectic would be quite impossible in view of the fact that his work—the result of seven decades of feverish activity—runs into many thousands of pages and embraces an enormous variety of topics. It is therefore necessary to single out a few central problems, even if this method carries with it the risk of over-simplification.

Two quotations from his works can be contrasted with each other as a point of departure. The first[1] emphasizes, in a dramatic tone of voice, that the outcome of the objective economic forces that dialectically clash with one another is open-ended, and as far as mankind is concerned everything depends on which of the opposite alternatives is realized by man himself:

> Whether the result of these objective determinants is the *highest level of humanity* or a *maximum of inhumanity*—this depends on us, this depends on human beings. Economic development cannot produce this by itself.

The second quotation,[2] by contrast, anticipates a positive solution. It goes as follows:

Even today, many obstacles remain. From the time of its birth, the revolutionary workers' movement has had to avoid ideological wrong-turnings of the most varied kind. So far, it has always succeeded in this, and it is my profound conviction that *it will succeed in future*. Allow me, then, to conclude this sketch with a somewhat modified saying of Zola : *"La vérité est lentement en marche et à la fin des fins rien ne l'arrêtera."*

The contradiction is striking; and yet it is more apparent than real. Here we are confronted with a central characteristic of Lukács' conception of dialectic. An attempt at elucidating and resolving this contradiction, to the extent to which it is possible to do the latter, is therefore a main task of this essay.

2. Early Development

It is always dangerous, if not arbitrary, to parcel up philosophers as "the young X" and "the mature X" for the sake of opposing one parcel to the other. The main outlines of a fundamental synthesizing idea not only may, but also must, be present in the philosopher's mind when he works out in a particular writing some of its concrete implications in particular contexts. This idea may, of course, undergo significant changes; the particular contexts themselves require constant re-elaborations and modifications in accordance with the specific characteristics of the concrete situations that have to be taken into account. But even a genuine conversion from "idealism" to "materialism" does not necessarily imply a radical rejection or repression of the original synthesizing idea.

A striking case in point in the twentieth century is Georg Lukács. His post-idealist works reveal in his approach to all major problems the same structure of thought, despite the fact that he had genuinely left behind his original idealistic positions. Those, however, who could not distinguish between the general structure of a philosopher's thought and its idealistic or materialistic articulation insisted that h "always remained a Hegelian idealist" and—follow ing their own preferences—either praised or blamed him for this. In doing so they were also implicitly ignoring the fact that Marx himself was a revolutionary well before he became a materialist, and he did not cease to be one afterwards.

It goes without saying that the continuity in question is a dialectical one: "the unity of continuity and discontinuity", i.e. the "supersession-preservation" (*Aufhebung*) of a previous stage in an increasingly higher complexity. Nevertheless it must be emphasized that there can be no originality without this—relative, dialectical—unity of thought as far as its general structure is concerned. For the precondition of any synthesis is some kind of synthesis as the active principle of selection of the first, even if the new synthesis apparently has nothing to do with the initial one. As Goethe said, "to be able to do something one must already be something",[3] which applies to the philosopher not less than to the artist or to anybody else. This is why one cannot properly understand a philosopher's thought without reaching down through its many layers to that original synthesis which structured it, dialectically, in all its successive modifications. (This is all the more important in cases —like Hegel, Marx, Lukács, Sartre, etc.—in which at some stage there seems to be a radical break with the past. But "radical break" is not the same as "qualitative change". The latter can characterize the totality of one's development, the former is confined to certain aspects of it, however important in some respects— e.g. sociologically—they might be. A "total conversion", in so far as it is not confined to the ideological content of one's thought but is claimed to embrace the person's general structure of thought, is very doubtful even as regards "religious fanatics". It is by no means accidental that disappointed religious communists turn into religious anti-communists. "Total conversion" is the privilege of a second intellectual infancy that may follow a total amnesia.)

Lukács' identification with Marxism signified a qualitative change in his development. It did not happen, however, overnight; it could not be characterized with the categories of "radical break" and "radically new" against which Lukács, in his defence of dialectic, waged a lifelong battle. On the contrary, the roots of this change ought to be sought a long way back, in his youthful dialectical synthesis and in its internal tensions. It can be no task of this essay to attempt to work out a typology of structures of thought in which Lukács could be situated. (The concepts that ought to be pursued in this respect range from "formalism", "monism", "dualism", "objectivism", "sub-jectivism", etc. to "fanaticism", "fatalism", "oppor-tunism", "oppositionalism", "rebelliousness", etc. etc.) It is necessary to stress, however, that we are not con-cerned here with some timeless psychological entity— a metaphysical fiction—but with a characterist¹ that can be explained only in concrete socio-hisorical terms. The formation of a philosopher's structure of thought has for its basis that ontological commitment —animated by a moral impetus—which is insepar-able from the issues of his particular situation. The trends of development which he perceives have their own "internal logic" and objective—though, of course, relative—continuity. This latter may, or may not, cor-respond to the dynamism of the philosopher's develop-ment. Rapid historical changes require greater and more radical adaptations through qualitatively differ-ing reassessments than relatively quiet and long drawn out transformations, and it is by no means certain that the individual is able to match the rhythm of historical dynamism. (The "conflict of generations" often has for its ground the inability of the older generation to readjust its own historical perspectives in accordance with some major changes which have occurred, or are about to emerge, and are perceived, however one-sidedly and with an unwarranted impression of finality, by the representatives of the younger generation.)

Yet: whatever the limits of adaptability of the

individual philosopher might be, the point is that he does not learn from books the important issues of his time, but lives them; that is, if he is a man of significance. Intellectual influences, therefore, ought to be treated with utmost care. For the significant philosopher follows Molière's advice in taking "son bien où il le trouve" and moulds all that which he has taken —not simply found—into a coherent whole of his own. Obviously here, again, the relationship is a dialectical one: it would be foolish to deny that the assimilated influences are *influences*, and have their effect on his further orientation as constitutive elements—though "*aufgehoben*" ones—of his principle of selection and synthesis. Nevertheless in this relationship the historical situation itself has the primacy over the intellectual influences. What separates the important philosopher from the clever eclectic is the historical irrelevance of the latter's merely academic synthesis as compared to the ultimate practical significance of the first.

The major influences on Lukács can be characterized with the following names: Georg Simmel, Wilhelm Dilthey, Emil Lask, Ervin Szabó, Georges Sorel, Heinrich Rickert (and other representatives of the Freiburg school of neo-Kantianism), Max Weber, Hegel, Marx, Rosa Luxemburg and Lenin. This list itself shows that the lion's share was taken by German culture, especially in the years of his intellectual formation. And yet, Lukács turned out to be the most radical critic of the internal contradictions of German thought and literature. A vast amount of his massive production is dedicated to the problems of German history and culture, but even the smallest article is written from a distance.[4] The backwardness of Hungarian philosophy left him no alternative to seeking orientation elsewhere, and attaching himself to the mainstream of German philosophy was, in the circumstances, the most obvious thing to do. The class into which he was born—the Hungarian Jewish bourgeoisie—was facing, at the time of Lukács' intellectual formation, a very complex situation. On the one hand, through its increasing economic power it was speedily emancipating itself in social standing from its subordination to the so-called "historical class"; on the other, it also succeeded in asserting its independence from the Austrian ruling classes. At the same time, however, it found itself confronted by a new social force: the challenge of the organized working-class movement. The belated development of Hungarian capitalism, the enormous inertia of feudal and bureaucratic-statal interests, the contradictions between the two major partners of the Austro-Hungarian monarchy, the special complications of Jewish emancipation, the increasing resistance of national minorities under Hungarian domination, these were the major factors in Lukács' situation. Many of his contemporaries, looking towards the west, simplified the tasks in the rather unrealistic programme of "bringing up to date" capitalistic Hungarian society. (Significantly, the two principal periodicals were called *The West* and *Twentieth Century*.) Lukács went a long step further : he emphasized the profound crisis of the bourgeoisie and its culture in general and thus conducted a constant polemic, even if in an indirect form, against the problematic and illusory character of the programme of "up-to-dating". As one of his first significant efforts he organized—at the age of nineteen—a theatre company called "Thalia" whose function was to bring culture to the working classes, which it did over a period of almost five years, until the frightened Hungarian Government's interference killed it. While Lukács fully recognized the great cultural-intellectual merits of both *The West* and *Twentieth Century*—he actively supported them with his regular contributions —he also realized the socio-political as well as philosophical limits of the trends expressed in them. Not only did he do this as a very young man, but also a great deal earlier than his intellectual contemporaries irrespective of age, with the exception of the syndicalist theoretician Ervin Szabó and the supremely great poet Endre Ady.

Here we reach a point of great importance : Lukács' relation to Ady. Their personal contacts were almost non-existent, so that Ady's impact on the young Lukács issued primarily from the reading of his poems. While his contemporaries were at odds with the intricately mediated meaning of Ady's symbolic poetry, recognizing in its author only the formal-linguistic innovator, the young Lukács was the first to focus attention on the organizing core of this poetry: the elemental passion of a democratic revolutionary.[5] The objective affinity of their search for a solution brought Lukács into the immediate vicinity of Ady, enabling him to grasp, already in its embryonic form, the true significance of a trend which was to become fully developed only several years later. Just as much as Ady, he felt the devastating inertia of the Hungarian situation in which the interaction of the heterogeneous contradictions mentioned above tended to emasculate all forces of social dynamism, maintaining the suffocating grip of conservative immobility. (It was still fresh in Lukács' memory that even their theatrical experiment was deemed dangerous by the guardians of the anachronistic *status quo*.) The rebellion against this kind of hopeless inertia and immobility had to take the form of pathetic denunciations, full of the cosmic undertones one finds in the "last warnings" of the prophets of doom; the more so since neither Ady nor Lukács' set against the inert anachronism of their situation, the equally (though in a different way) anachronistic ideal of bourgeois stability so dear to the heart of the anglophile Don Quixotes of the western-orientated Hungarian bourgeoisie.

Ady's sombre prophetic Messianism, with its dramatic appeals formulated in terms of "*either* salvation *or* total disaster*", expressed with the highest lyric intensity the dilemmas of those who, in their efforts to find a solution to their particular problems on a European scale, had to perceive the deepening crisis of the social order on a global scale. How simple it was, by comparison, for Petöfi when, in 1848-9 and before, he could appeal to the example of France in his programme, aiming at the radical overcoming of Hungarian feudalism: the clear and straightforward character of his poetry bears witness to this. For Ady, however, there was no alternative to singing in this voice:

> Saltier are the tears here,
> And the pains hurt more.
> The Magyar Messiahs are Messiahs
> A thousand times, and more.
>
> They die a thousand deaths,
> But their crosses bring no salvation,
> For they could do nothing,
> They were condemned to achieve naught.

What could be set against such inertia of powerlessness? Only a dramatic appeal to an "*ought*" emerging from the succession of heightened alternatives:

> New flames, new faiths, new furnaces, new saints,
> Either you are real, or vanish again in the mist of
> nothing.

> Either this faith of ours turns into reality,
> Or, bereft of reason, we are doomed to the last.

Thirty years after the publication of his first essay on Ady, Lukács quoted the lines:

> Will it last long, still longer
> The old fate, the old curse?
> *Lingering, inert, red Sun*
> *I implore Thee.*

and commented: "for Ady the democratic revolution existed, and could only exist, as *desire, hope and dream*".[6] He might have written the same words about the young Lukács. Their perspectives were essentially the same in a fundamental respect: in that the solution could appear on their horizon only in the form of an "ought", articulated in alternatives of the utmost dramatic intensity. The poetic qualities of the young Lukács' style—*The Soul and the Forms, Aesthetic Culture, The Theory of the Novel*—which were to disappear later, find their explanation in these perspectives, in this horizon. In the course of the 1917-18 social upheavals his perspectives changed, and what was earlier a "desire, hope and dream" turned for him into a concrete, practical task, representing a "scientific challenge" directly associated with the tangible issues of economic and social organization and programming. At this point the old style had to give way to the matter-of-fact, prosaic, practice-orientated style of a peculiar brand of economic-philosophical and politico-historical reasoning.

3. Change of Perspective

And yet, the supersession of the youthful perspectives remained a relative one. As we shall see later, the concern for "ought" and the enunciation of dramatic alternatives has remained with Lukács ever since. His identification with Marxism has given, it goes without saying, a qualitatively new setting to this concern. The stylistic change went parallel to the transference of "ought" to a different level, and it was by no means achieved overnight. (*History and Class Consciousness* is his major work of transition, preceded by essays like *Bolshevism as a Moral Problem, Tactics and Ethics, The Role of Morality in Communist Production*, etc., which shows as regards both style and issues a significant affinity with his earlier works. The book on *Lenin*, written in 1924, is markedly different in this respect.) The problems associated with "ought" have become progressively mediated in his works—Lukács would say "concretized"—and topics have been brought into the foreground which have apparently very little to do with "ought", save in the form of negative polemics. Nevertheless his original confrontation with *"Sollen"*, with "ought", has remained a fundamental structuring dimension of Lukács' entire thought.

It cannot be stressed enough: we are not concerned with the influences of neo-Kantianism, etc. The young Lukács reached out for them in the spirit of his own situation and assimilated them in his own way, in a comprehensive synthesis not in the least recognizable in the work of any one of his friends and teachers. Max Weber, to name but the most significant of them, was well aware of the impressive originality of the young Hungarian philosopher, and regarded him more as an intellectual equal than a pupil. As we have seen in his relation to Ady, the overriding factor was the common objective situation—the perception of which produced a profound affinity of perspectives.

Paradoxical as it might seem, the historical backwardness of Hungarian development proved to be the vantage point of a profoundly original synthesis. It was not simply that Hungary was socially backward. Russia was on the whole no more advanced, but in her development she was catching up with the most advanced countries in socio-political dynamism. In a complex historical situation it is never simply the economic and social maturity of a given country that is the cause of radical changes but the favourable configuration of the various causal factors into a dynamic overall pattern.[7] Both Russia and China have amply proved this point. Hungary, by contrast, was characterized by a very different overall configuration. In that country there were many forms of ideological and political movements, from reactionary conservatism to liberalism, from populism to Marxist-orientated syndicalism, and from nationalism to bourgeois radicalism. Their interactions, however, because of the underlying objective stalemate of the heterogeneous social contradictions, could only emphasize the massiveness of general social impotence and immobility. Those who rebelled against the latter had to aim—in ideological terms—at the transcendence of all the existing forms of impotence-enhancing partial opposition. This rebellion took place with various degrees of socio-philosophical awareness and political radicalism. Nevertheless a concern for universality was an integral part of it. It produced not only some peaks of twentieth-century European culture—like Ady, Lukács, Bartók, Kodály, and Attila József—but also an almost incredible number of outstanding individuals in every field of culture and across the whole spectrum of ideology.[8]

As to Lukács, the possibility of transformation was conceived by him in terms of "either a complete fulfilment or no substantial change at all". When, in his

youth, he turned away from the perspectives of socialism he did this with the justification that although
"the only hope could be in the proletariat, in socialism
. . . it seems that socialism does not possess the religious
power which is capable of filling the entire soul: a
power that characterized primitive Christianity".[9]
The measure and magnitude of expectations was set
in these terms and when in 1917-18 he identified himself with socialist perspectives he did not give up an
iota from the radicalism and totality of this measure.
This is where we can see clearly the essential continuity of his development in a dialectical sense: i.e.
the reformulation of an all-pervasive conception in
terms of a new social instrumentality. Of course the
change of perspectives took place in the middle of a
grave international crisis—the end of the First World
War and the October Revolution—which he observed
from a rather inert national setting. Even after the
Hungarian revolutionary events it remained true that
in the country there existed no powerful social agency
which could have materialized the changes desired
and advocated by Lukács. Understandably, therefore,
his social philosophy bears the marks of the socio-
political vacuum to which it was related, in sharp
contrast to the tremendous realism that characterized
almost every single line of Lenin's writing. Lenin
reads even Hegel's *Logic*—in the interval between
two revolutions—in order to derive concrete stimuli
for the solution of the urgent immediate *practical* tasks

he faces in planning and organizationally preparing the October revolution. Lukács reads even Lenin in order to concretize, but always in *theoretical* terms, his own general philosophical synthesis. Lukács repeatedly postulates the unity of theory and practice; Lenin lives it in a specific form. But such contrasts cannot be simply explained with reference to differences, real or alleged, in intellectual talents. References of this kind rather beg the question, ignoring the fact that the realized intellectual talent is the result of the interaction between whatever gifts the individual might have had and his situation. The striking contrasts are basically due to the fact that while Lenin's entire predicament is dense with concrete practical tasks, Lukács' practical possibilities can only be compared to a rarefied atmosphere. Even at the time of the shortlived Hungarian revolution of 1919 the margin of real possibilities is almost infinitesimal as compared to the magnitude of the tasks and problems. The old inertia, helped by the international situation in the aftermath of the October revolution, prevailed again, "condemning to achieve naught" those who tried to rebel against it. And the political movement of an emigration which lacks a solid backing in its own country of origin is, in practical terms, but the original rarefied atmosphere still more rarefied.

This situation has given an ambivalent character to Lukács' perspectives. If he wanted to render more

concrete his general conception, in an effort of translating it into a feasible practical programme for him,
there was no alternative to associating himself with
the increasingly more Stalinist-dominated Communist
International. (Although he remained always in an
internal opposition both in his Party and in ʰhe
Comintern, he could not avoid, as we shall see, ʿhe
problematic effects of this association however necessary it was.) On the other hand the weakness of the
practical-political predicament also turned into an
advantage for him. It enabled him to tackle and
elaborate some fundamental philosophical categories
of the greatest ultimate practical significance—e.g.
"totality" and "mediation" (*Vermittlung*), to be discussed later. It also enabled him to anticipate the
objective logic of Stalinistic developments as early as
the spring of 1919, in the framework of a general theoretical consideration into which he has "trans-substan-
tiated" an immediate and, as far as the Hungarian
circumstances were concerned, hopeless practical task.
The issue is important enough to warrant the long
quotation that follows:[10]

It is clear that the most oppressive phenomena of
proletarian power—namely, scarcity of goods and
high prices, of whose immediate consequences every
proletarian has personal experience—are direct consequences of the slackening of labour-discipline and
the decline in production. The creation of remedies
for these, and the consequent improvement in the

individual's standard of living, can only be brought about when the causes of these phenomena have been removed. Help comes in two ways. Either the individuals who constitute the proletariat *realize* that they can help themselves only by bringing about a voluntary strengthening of labour-discipline, and consequently a rise in production; or, if they are incapable of this, *they create institutions which are capable of bringing about this necessary state of affairs.* In the latter case, they create a legal system through which the proletariat *compels* its own individual members, the proletarians, to act in a way which corresponds to their class-interests : *the proletariat turns its dictatorship against itself.* This measure is necessary for the self-preservation of the proletariat when correct recognition of class-interests and voluntary action in these interests do not exist. But one must not hide from oneself the fact that *this method contains within itself great dangers for the future.* When the proletariat itself is the creator of labour-discipline, when the labour-system of the proletarian state is built on a *moral* basis, then the external compulsion of the law ceases *automatically* with the abolition of class-division—that is, the state withers away—and this liquidation of class-division produces out of itself the beginning of the true history of humanity, which Marx prophesied and hoped for. If, on the other hand, the proletariat follows another path, it must create a legal system which cannot be abolished automatically by historical development. Development would therefore proceed in a direction *which endangered the appearance and realization of the ultimate aim.* For the legal system which the proletariat is compelled to create in this way *must be overthrown*—and who knows what convulsions and what injuries will be caused by a transition which leads from the kingdom of necessity to the kingdom of freedom by such a *détour?* . . . It depends on the proletariat whether the real history of humanity begins—that is to say, *the power of morality over institutions and economics.*

This quotation gives clear expression to practical and political misery in the shape of an abstract moral postulate—the moralizing direct appeal to the consciousness of the proletariat.[11] It also shows Lukács' great power of insight as regards the objective dialectic of a certain type of development. Lenin, by comparison, was far too busy squeezing out the last drop of practical socialist possibilities from the objective instrumental set-up of his situation to indulge in theoretical anticipations of this kind in 1919. By the time he started to concentrate on the dreadful danger of Stalinistic bureaucratization and the prevalence of the "institutions of necessity" over the ideals of socialism it was too late. It is pathetic to see Lenin, a genius of realistic strategy, behaving like a desperate utopian from 1923 to the moment of his death, insistently putting forward hopeless schemes—like the proposal to create a majority in the Central Committee from working-class cadres in order to neutralize the Party bureaucrats—in the hope of reversing this dangerous trend, by now far too advanced. Lenin's great tragedy was that his incomparable, instrumentally concrete, intensely practical strategy in the end defeated him.

In the last year of his life there was no longer a way
out of his almost total isolation : the development he
himself, far above anybody else, had helped to set in
motion had made him historically superfluous. The
specific form in which he lived the unity of theory
and practice proved to be the limit even of his greatness.

In this issue we find manifest the general dilemma
of the relationship between Politics and Philosophy.
We shall return later to this question. In this connection the point to be stressed is that Lukács defined
his own position in the unhappy correlation between
direct practical instrumentality as manifest in the
Soviet developments—the only *real* one over a long
historical period, whatever its contradictions—and the
universal perspectives of socialism in general. He
attempted the impossible task of bridging the gap
between the two, not out of selfish opportunism—one
can hardly imagine a more selfless person than him,
as has been recognized even by his political opponents[12]—but because of the objective external and
internal limitations of his general position. The practical rarefaction of his own political predicament and
the limitations of the instrumentality of "Socialism in
one country" forced him to focus attention on the far-
away perspectives of "soul-filling socialism". Paradoxically this also enabled him to identify and elaborate some general issues of the greatest ultimate
practical significance that were hardly, if ever, noticed

before him. At the same time, in the course of his efforts to indicate the concrete social agencies which could translate his ultimate perspectives into practical reality, the internal logic of his general position has more than once compelled him to take for a solution something that was far from it. (His references to the "asiatic form of socialism" amounted to no more than pinpointing the handicaps Soviet society should get rid of in order to remain the model of socialist development.) Thus the two poles of his thought reciprocally conditioned each other, often producing in his syntheses an abstract immediacy on the one hand and a pseudo-concreteness on the other, in so far as far-away perspectives were transferred by him into the present or near future. (Especially in his writings on People's Democracy.)

Not that he was unaware of the gap between the given practical instrumentality and the general perspectives. He spent by far the greatest amount of his energies in trying to work out those "mediations" which should bridge that gap. (The numerous works he has written in the course of his never-ending confrontation with the problem of mediation (*Vermittlung*) acquire their full meaning only in this connection.) He never ceased to talk about the task of "overcoming" (*Überwindung*). But his "*Überwindung*" could never be other than a *theoretical* one on the premise of the theoretical—not merely tactical—acceptance of the instrumental validity of "Socialism in one country". Although later he greatly improved upon his just-quoted position, he has never fully realized that the alternative between "free insight, producing voluntary activity" and "the institutions of necessity" is a hopelessly abstract and, therefore, false alternative; that one form of instrumentality can realistically be opposed only by another form of instrumentality and institutions. He tried, instead, an "*Überwindung*" in the form of a synthesis between the "free insight" and "necessity"—in his theory of the "Leninist Party" as the "bearer of proletarian class-consciousness"[13]—and thus in his "ought-ridden" abstract-theoretical solution of the problem ended up with idealizing an "institution of necessity". The possible alternatives which objectively implied the revision of his premise had to remain completely outside his horizon. (It is highly significant that the profoundly original perspectives of both Gramsci and Mao Tse-tung, despite their massive implications for the development of the socialist movement as a whole, have found no positive resonance whatsoever[14] in a man of such intellect and sensitivity as Lukács. His one-sided judgments on Trotsky find their explanation in the same limitations.)

That the validity of Lukács' perspectives as attached to a narrow instrumentality is historically superseded is obvious enough. What needs repeated emphasis is that his perspectives are characterized by a dialectical bipolarity. As we have seen, not only the problem-

39

atically-immediate—i.e. the already superseded—conditioned the "far-away perspectives", but also the latter determined his interpretation of the concrete situations and of their significance. This means not only that the critical assessment of his works, including the most polemical ones, requires the constant awareness of the historical circumstances and dialectical interconnections. It also means that one should look out for those aspects of his *oeuvre* which, due to the historical validity of many of his long-term formulations, represent a deep-rooted, concrete, topical as well as enduring achievement. For this complex bipolarity of his perspectives has provided him with a margin of activity that enabled him to produce—primarily in the "mediated" field of Aesthetics and in the more abstract spheres of Philosophy—works of exemplary value.

4. "Ought" and Objectivity

Lukács' concept of "*Sollen*", or "ought", is far more complex than it would seem at first sight. The dominant note of his formulations (*Fragestellungen*) is a "longing for objectivity" and, in accordance with it, a never-ending explicit polemic against "ought". Yet he is intensely aware of the problematic character of any cult of objectivity in our age, and therefore qualifies his statements in such a way that the "overtones" of his analyses to some extent reassert the validity of "ought" in an indirect form. This is why his attitude must remain a "*longing for* objectivity", and never an unproblematic self-identification with it—whether under the heading of the category of "life" (*Lebensphilosophie*) or of those of "economic reality", "productive forces", "class", "history", etc.

Also, this is why already the young Lukács feels the greatest sympathy for Thomas Mann who remains his twentieth-century literary hero ever since. In an essay written in 1909, after praising Mann's dialectical and artistic power of seeing "the connection between all things" (*den Zusammenhang von allem mit allem*) as well as his great sense of objectivity, Lukács makes the general point that "objectivity can perhaps never exist without a certain irony. The most serious regard for things is always somewhat ironic, for somewhere or other the great gulf between cause and effect, between the conjuring of fate and the fate conjured, must become obvious. And the more natural the peaceful flow of things appears, the truer and deeper this irony will be. Admittedly it is only in *Buddenbrooks* that this emerges so clearly and, as it were, from a single source. In the later writings this irony of Mann takes on differing forms, yet its deepest root remains this feeling of dislocation from, and longing for, the great natural vegetative community".[15] The philosopher feels the same dislocation from, and the same longing for, an objective synthesis and unity in a world in which the gulf between "cause and effect", "intention and result", "value and reality" (*Wert und Wirklichkeit*) appears to be ever increasing, although of course for him "irony" cannot bring a solution. And whatever the envisaged particular solution may be, throughout all its modifications in the course of Lukács' development the underlying original programmatic challenge remains a major structuring factor of his thought for the rest of his life.

Lukács' entire work is characterized by incessant
attempts at finding a way of removing the tragic
menace implicit in the "either—or" situation (the
possibility of the dominion of "a maximum of inhum-
anity"). His "longing for objectivity" is in the spirit
of a constant struggle against "bad objectivity". From
the very beginning he realizes that a direct appeal to
"Sollen" ("obligation") on the lines of *"Individual-
ethik"* ("Individual ethics"), is hopelessly inadequate,
and therefore he opposes to it the imperative of some
objective force. But the "unity", the "supersession of
opposites"—if claimed at all—is built on an imperatival foundation. Thus *"der Zweispalt von Sein und
Sollen ist nicht aufgehoben"*—"the division between
'is' and 'ought' is not transcended". It is only given a
dialectical, and increasingly more concrete, assessment.

The reason for this can be found in a certain
duality in Lukács' conception of Ontology. Even the
most recent Lukács—the author of a massive *Social
Ontology*—insists on a duality, on a dual causality,
and on an ultimate autonomy of "decisions between
alternatives" (*Alternativentscheidungen*). The gist of
his argument is as follows:

There are causal connections which work *as spon-
taneous causes*, and there are causal connections
which are set in motion in a specific way by a teleo-
logical initiative, whereby they still preserve their
causal necessity . . . I come now to another basic
ontological problem of social development, which is

linked with the fact that society is an extraordinarily complicated complex of complexes, in which there are two opposite poles. On the one hand there is the *totality of society*, which ultimately determines the interactions of the individual complexes, and on the other there is the complex individual man, who constitutes an *irreducible minimal unity* within the process. By their interaction, these poles determine the process. In this process, man finally becomes man; . . . the aspect of freedom acquires a significance which is ever greater, ever more comprehensive, embracing the whole of humanity . . . I assert, therefore, that however much all these problems have been made possible by economic factors, they can be translated into reality only through men's *decisions between* alternatives.[16]

The *purely objective development* of labour creates, it is true, an ever-diminishing minimum of necessary labour; but that it is capable of turning labour into a need of life is not part of this ontology. Rather, at a determinate stage, men must make labour a need of life.[17]

The question is not whether one agrees with Lukács or not. It is rather that on the basis of his Ontology the positive outcome can only be envisaged as the impact of a "*Sollen*"; the autonomous choice of their potential humanity by the individuals (the "*irreducible minimal unities*") who become aware, after an arduous work of theoretical demonstration and persuasion, that they *can* and *ought to* change their way of life :

It must be one of our major tasks to offer a theoretical proof of the fact that all these circumstances and reifications are only phenomenal forms of real processes. By this, we shall *gradually make men understand* that they *ought* to experience their own life too as an historical process.

It is important therefore, *to awaken* the *genuinely* independent personality, whose *possibility* has been created by previous economic development.[19]

And here we arrive at the question of resolving in so far as it is possible, the apparent contradiction referred to at the beginning of this essay. If the objective development produces "open-ended" alternatives, clearly there can be no other power to bring about the desired solution than the "work of consciousness upon consciousness". (This, in Lukács' eyes, opens up a great field of activity for the intellectual—also putting a tremendous moral responsibility[20] on his shoulders.) If, however, this work of illumination and persuasion is to succeed, it cannot do without the assertion that "*la vérité est lentement en marche et à la fin des fins rien ne l'arrêtera*".

5. Continuity and Discontinuity

So far the stress has been laid mainly on the unity of
Lukács' thought; now it is necessary to show, however briefly, the inner logic of his development: the
modifications of his position within the ultimate unity
and the determinations behind them. In the confines
of this essay there is no space for more than bare outlines. But however summary and schematic the result
may be, it is necessary to trace them in order not to
distort the overall picture.[21]

The Soul and the Forms—a volume of essays
written between 1908 and 1910—is Lukács' first major
intellectual achievement. It is a work of great sensitivity, dense with allusions and inexhaustible ambi-
guities. It has no unifying topic, and yet the overall
impression is that of having read *one* work, not an
occasional collection of essays. (Lukács' post-1913
collections are very different indeed in this respect.)

47

The compositional principle of these early essays—including those which make up *Aesthetic Culture*—is heavily weighed down on the subjective side. The chosen topics are more grounds for a "take-off" than objective points of reference. Paradoxically it is the absence of a sharply defined central theme that unites these essays, not its presence. Only the partial themes are well lit and properly in focus. But the dialectical contrasts of the sharply focused partial themes produce an overall *chiaroscuro* effect: that of a vaguely contoured, unresolved complexity. One might say that these essays are "variations on a missing theme". The synthesizing theme—which is originally there only as a vague intuition, as an undefined and inarticulate "longing for objectivity"—is being born before our eyes. As it takes shape through its partial aspects, bringing into life at the same time the challenge of the supersession of that partiality, it foreshadows the necessary destruction of the young Lukács' essay form.

The question of fragmentation appears time and again, under many of its aspects. "Human knowledge," writes Lukács, "is a *psychological nihilism. We see a thousand relations, yet never grasp a genuine connection. The landscapes of our soul exist nowhere; yet in them, every tree and every flower is concrete.*"[22] Again, "The man of George's lyrics . . . is a solitary man, freed from all social ties."[23] And again:

48

Kassner sees *syntheses* only, as it were, with his eyes closed; when he looks at things he sees so much, such delicate details, so much that can never be repeated, that *every synthesis must appear as a lie,* as a deliberate falsification. If he gives in to his longing, if he closes his eyes so that he can see things *together—in the realm of values—*his honesty immediately compels him to look at them again, and once more they are separated, isolated, without air. The oscillation between these two poles determines Kassner's style.[24]

When, against such a background, he says of the George poems that "One day, perhaps, even these poems could become folk-songs",[25] that amounts to nothing more than a gratuitous hope : the weakest of all possible "oughts ". Nevertheless, this does not alter in the least the fact that the challenge itself has appeared on the horizon, carrying with it the growing realization that there can be no solution in terms of value-postulates. Lukács sets out to find solutions to partial problems. He finds none, but emerges victorious from his defeat. For what he achieves is the metamorphosis of his original problems into a qualitatively higher complex of more concrete questions. Armed with the graphic awareness that the concreteness of the "trees and flowers devoid of landscape" is a meaningless concreteness, he is now in a position to attack the all-important issue of "totality". The price he has to pay for this unintended achievement is the definitive abandoning of the early essay form, with all the immediate attractiveness attached to it.

The consummation of this essay form takes place in *The Theory of the Novel*, in 1914-15. It was originally intended as an introduction to a massive systematic work that has never been brought to completion. (Hundreds of pages of manuscript exist deliberately unpublished: Lukács once described to me this attempt of his at a systematization as a "six-legged monster".)[26] It turned out to be a great accomplished essay *malgré lui*. The appearance of systematization in *The Theory of the Novel* should not deceive us: the real structure—the fundamental compositional principle—is essayistic, in the spirit of the early essay form. The analysed works do not preserve their own physiognomy; they are "sublimated" into pillars of an intellectual (a "*geisteswissenschaftliche*") construction. The full potentiality of the early essay form is brought to its fulfilment and stretched to its extreme limits in *The Theory of the Novel*, due to the qualitatively higher complex of problems it sets out to solve as compared with the earlier volumes. In the course of its fulfilment, however, this early essay form is also made to burst, and thus it is permanently transcended in Lukács' development. The element of objectivity—in the *Problematik* of "totality" inherited from *The Soul and the Forms*—floods it and proves to be far too massive for its fragile structure. There will be no more return to it, nor could there be; only occasional expressions of a feeling of *nostalgia* for a necessarily and (in Lukács' view) rightly lost formal accomplishment. The peculiar appeal of *The Theory of the Novel* is inseparable from the historical resonance of a widespread feeling of nostalgia for the accomplishment displayed in it. *The Theory of the Novel* is *no longer* within the bounds of a (disciplined) subjectivity, and *not yet* the conscious acceptance of the methodological impersonality that follows from the recognition of the ultimate determining power of "objective totality". (This means also the conscious subordination of one's compositional aspirations to the task of tracing the chaotic intricacies and "orderless" complexities of the objective order.) It is a once-only work which is characterized by the contradiction between the highest intensity of awareness of the power of objectivity, and the uncompromising radicalism of its rejection. The unique appeal of this work is that the contradiction is "transcended" in it —if only subjectively—through formal accomplishment, compositional rigour, poetic imagery and passionately heightened style.[27] Ideologically it is situated in some sort of a "limbo" immediately at the confines of the vision of a capitalistic hell. No wonder that the champions of a romanticized limbo of intellectual existence have turned it into their myth.

The "new world-epoch" (*neue Weltepoche*) that appears on the horizon of *The Theory of the Novel* is no more than a vague intuition: even in the final references to Dostoevsky it remains a mysterious hint, an ought-ridden question mark. It is forced into the picture by the inner dialectic of his arguments, by the realization that:

> The process which constitutes the inner form of the novel is the problematic individual's journey to himself; the road from gloomy captivity in reality which merely exists, which is heterogeneous and is meaningless for the individual—the road from this to clear self-knowledge. When this self-knowledge is attained, the ideal that has been discovered does, it is true, appear in the midst of life as the meaning of life; but *the division between "is" and "ought" is not transcended*, and cannot be transcended in the sphere in which this is enacted, namely in the life-sphere of the novel.[28]

Nevertheless when in the unfinished manuscript Lukács tries further to concretize this problem of *"Aufhebung"* within the confines of his vision of this period, he finds that he never gets beyond a cancerously growing work leading nowhere. This manuscript is characterized by enormously long "run-ups" to jumps materializing in landings right on the spot of the "take-off". The significance of this unfinishable manuscript for Lukács' development was that it intensified his awareness—which he felt even at this level of abstraction—of being right in the middle of a blind alley. One of the maxims Lukács used to recommend was: "do not stop half-way but follow uncompromisingly the idea to its conclusion; the sparks produced by the collision of your head with the wall will show you that you have reached the limits". He learned it from Georg Simmel, in his "privatissimo" seminar, and accepted it as both subjectively and objectively valid. He never experienced a higher intensity of sparks than in this period of the unfinished synthesis, but he fully explored in all directions the limits of adaptability of the Hegelian categories. His unpublished manuscript graphically displays the inadequacy of these categories for coping with the specific complexities of our historical situation, despite the passionate efforts of a great intellect to bring them "up-to-date". For this reason alone, if not for others, it well deserves to see the light of the day.

The deep personal crisis was helped to a solution by the dramatic intensification of events: the October Revolution, the military collapse of the Austro-Hungarian Monarchy and the eruption of a general socio-economic and political crisis. Seeing the "new world-epoch" of *The Theory of the Novel* emerging as a concrete material force, he hailed it with enthusiasm and with great immediate expectations. His first attempts at a radical reassessment bear the marks of an impatient, hasty unification—in theory—of the newly identified material force and his principle of a morally founded practical synthesis. The way he greets the unification of the Hungarian Communist and Social Democratic Parties is highly characteristic of this mood:

Today the (unified) party is the expression of the unified will of the unified proletariat; it is the executive organ of the will which is forming itself out of new forces in the new society. The crisis of socialism, which was expressed by the *dialectical opposition between the two types of workers' parties*, has at last reached its end. The proletarian movement has *finally* entered upon a new phase, the phase of its power. The mighty deed of the Hungarian proletariat consists in the fact that it has finally led the world revolution into this new phase. The Russian revolution has shown that the proletariat is able to take power and to organize a new society. The Hungarian revolution has shown that this revolution is possible without fratricidal strife between proletarians. With this, the world revolution reaches an increasingly advanced stage. It redounds to the honour of the Hungarian proletariat that it has been able to create *from itself* the power necessary for this leading role—for *leading its leaders, and the proletarians of all countries*.[29]

Similarly, as we have already seen (pp. 34–6), the solution of a well identified dilemma of socialist power is envisaged in terms of a moral postulate versus institutions. The early destruction of the Hungarian experiment put an understandable end to this mood. There follows afterwards a passionate *prise de conscience* of the highest intellectual intensity, whose rightly famous—though often misunderstood or misinterpreted—monument is *History and Class-Consciousness*. This work is not only a profoundly original

and largely successful attempt at a Marxist supersession of Hegel (apart from certain aspects of the thorny
issue of "Subject-Object"—relations), but also raises
a host of concrete institutional and organizational
problems in close conjunction with the most general
philosophical ones. E.g. :

> The Workers' Council is the *politico-social conquest
> of capitalist reification.* In the situation after the
> dictatorship, it ought to overcome the bourgeois
> separation of legislative, executive and judiciary;
> similarly, in the struggle for power it is called upon
> to end the spatio-temporal fragmentation of the pro-
> letariat, and also to bring together economics and
> politics into the true unity of proletarian activity, and
> in this way *to help to reconcile the dialectical opposi-
> tion of immediate interest and ultimate aim.*[30]

Thus although the imperatival element is still very
strong, the recognition of the mediatory potential of
a historically concrete institution is a significant step
forward from the earlier position.

In the twenties Lukács' energies are divided between
political tasks and philosophical studies. In politics his
position is by no means a happy one, receiving attack
after attack from Comintern functionaries and sectarian leaders of his own Party. And after the defeat
of his "Blum theses" even his peripheral political
activity comes to a close. From then onwards his
activity is confined to theoretical work and, during
a short interval after the war in Hungary again, to the

politics of culture. The philosophical studies, in the form of closely argued reviews, carry on the investigations left off in *History and Class-Consciousness*. (The most important of them are the articles on Bukharin, Lassalle and Moses Hess. The little book on Lenin is in a class of its own, characterized by a clear synthesis of some central problems of dialectic—elaborated in *History and Class-Consciousness*—with a remarkable sense of political reality.) One can notice in them the impact of a growing assimilation of political economy, though the peak in this respect is represented by a major systematic work written in the thirties: *The Young Hegel, On the Relations between Dialectic and Economics*. (As a programme the central theme of this book first appears in *Moses Hess and the Problems of Idealistic Dialectic*.)

The thirties bring back the literary essays but, of course, in a fundamentally different form. As to their structure, they are much closer to the systematic monograph than to the traditional essay. Their composition is dictated by the objective connections of the works analyzed as seen in the general framework of Lukács' conception of the world, however complex and "side-tracking" they might be. The author of these essays takes upon himself the task of tackling problems which the young Lukács would have *a priori* excluded from his field of interest. The central notion that both guides these essays and emerges from them in an increasingly more concrete form is the concept of "specific". Its universal philosophical equivalent—"mediation"—has been repeatedly tackled in the preceding period. Without the successful tackling of this general problem the new literary essays would have been devoid of a principle of internal cohesion which could ultimately prevail over their manifold ramifications and involved complexities. On the ground of this general point of reference Lukács was enabled not only to plunge into the most heterogeneous aspects of the works of art discussed—from the political and sociological ones to the moral and epistemological aspects—as they presented themselves in their concrete individuality, but also to synthesize them into a well-identifiable particular aesthetic picture. As the field of his concrete investigation enlarged, so his general aesthetic categories gained in concreteness and complexity. Thus the "condensed monographs" have dialectically prepared the ground for a general aesthetic synthesis as well.

By the time, however, that he could start writing the latter, important changes in the world perspectives of socialism—the programme of "destalinization", the Hungarian explosion, China and later Cuba, etc. —brought with them new complications. They brought out into the open a latent contradiction in Lukács' essays. For the intense "mediatedness" that characterizes them is by no means simply an adequate fusion with the specific character of the works he discusses, although to a lastingly significant extent it is that too. It is at the same time also an *"incognito"* for politico-philosophical polemics into which he has been pushed as a result of his forced retirement from politics and the hardening conditions of life under Stalin, as well as a resignation to the narrowing down of perspectives and to the inevitability of what he called a "historically necessary *détour*". In so far as the "side-trackings" in his literary analyses are due to this "incognito" and "resignation", his own objective compositional principle of the essays is evidently violated, no matter how important the excursions themselves might be in other respects. (All the more because some important formal aspects of the analysed works are inevitably pushed into the background in the course of such incursions and excursions.) More important, however, is the fact that the preparatory work to the later synthesis turns out, even in the light of Lukács' own perception of the changing perspectives, to be temporally conditioned to a more than acceptable extent. One of the measures of Lukács' greatness is that he finds the moral strength and intellectual power to face up to the challenge of a "new beginning", even past the age of seventy.

There is here a more than superficial similiarity to the crisis of the *Theory of the Novel* period, even if coupled with essential differences. The first result of his attempt at a synthesis is the book *On Particularity as a Category of Aesthetics* (*Über die Besonderheit als Kategorie der Ästhetik*). It was planned

originally as an Introduction to the major aesthetic
work. As it turned out, it had to be kept separate from
the latter. The essential difference from the years
around 1915 is, however, that the new personal crisis
—again, against the background of an objective historical crisis—has been attacked and resolved, to the
extent that it was possible for him so far, within the
perspectives of Marxism. This fact has enabled him
to complete the new work; the massive volumes of
Die Eigenart des Ästhetischen. But this work clearly
bears the marks of an unresolved situation : it is much
more like a *"Rohentwurf"* (rough draft) than an
accomplished synthesis. It reveals heterogeneous layers
of the development of his thought, left side by side.
Also, the extensive new "groundwork"—made necessary by the realization of the temporal shortcomings
of the earlier preparations as well as by an acute
awareness of the unfilled gaps—is being done in front
of our eyes and incorporated in its immediacy into
the general synthesis. This latter characteristic—and
not the level of abstraction—sadly cuts off this fundamental work from the reading public.[31] Another
major work of searching re-examination and synthesis
is the just completed *Ontology of Social Being*, known
so far only from Lukács' own account of it. On the
evidence of the latter one can only hope, but by no
means anticipate, that the completed work itself succeeds in superseding the internally determined
"Rohentwurf" character of his *Aesthetic*.

6. Totality and Mediation

The central categories of Lukács' dialectic are the closely interrelated concepts of "totality" and "mediation". Adequate discussion of them would require a very detailed analysis which is, unfortunately, out of the question here. We have to content ourselves, again, with tracing the bare outlines of Lukács' formulations and solutions of these problems.

As we have seen, the passionate revolt of the young Lukács against the prevailing forms of capitalistic fragmentation and isolationism had brought with it very early expectations as regards a possible solution, and postulates of an uncompromisingly comprehensive character. But we have also seen that even in *The Theory of the Novel* the concept of totality remained an abstract regulative principle, despite the heightened awareness of its crucial importance. It was in *History and Class-Consciousness* that Lukács first succeeded in raising, at the highest level of generalization, the issue of "concrete totality".

He emphasized that

> It is not the predominance of economic motives in the interpretation of society which is the decisive difference between Marxism and bourgeois science, but rather *the point of view of totality.* The category of totality, the all-round, determining *domination of the whole over the parts* is the essence of the method which Marx took over from Hegel and, in an original manner, *transformed* into the basis of an entirely new science.[32]

And he added, after his criticism of the "individual standpoint" of bourgeois theory: *"The totality of the object* can be posited only when *the positing subject* is itself a totality".[33] Although the opposition of "individual standpoint" and "the standpoint of totality" is still an abstract one, it enables him to work out the Social Ontology of *History and Class-Consciousness.* He asserts that *"Concrete totality* is therefore the *true category of reality",*[34] and concretizes it as "socio-historical process" (*gesellschaftliches Geschehen*),[35] and formulates the task of the supersession of the theoretical-intellectual-artistic fragmentation as a necessary dimension of the practical unification of "Subject and Object". (When, in the already quoted recent work, he defines social totality as a "complex of complexes", he offers a much more concrete general framework of reference which promises an *Ontology* far superior to that of *History and Class-Consciousness*.)

However, "social totality" without "mediation" is rather like "freedom without equality": an abstract —and empty—postulate. "Social totality" exists in and through those manifold mediations through which the specific complexes—i.e. "partial totalities"—are linked to each other in a constantly shifting and changing, dynamic overall complex. The direct cult of totality, the mystification of totality as an immediacy, the negation of mediations and complex interconnections with each other, can only produce a myth and, as Nazism has proved, a dangerous one at that. The other extreme of undialectical separation: the cult of immediacy and the negation of totality, of the objective interconnections between the individual complexes, is also dangerous, producing disorientation, the defence of fragmentation, the psychology of the meaninglessness of one's actions, the cynical rejection of morally inspired activity, and the powerless acceptance of one's conditions, however inhuman they might be. No wonder that Lukács rejects them both.

His "tertium datur" is a historically concrete, dialectical conception of totality. He writes in 1947: "The materialist-dialectical conception of totality means *first* of all the concrete unity of interacting contradictions . . .; *secondly, the systematic relativity* of all totality both *upwards* and *downwards* (which means that all totality is made of totalities *subordin-ated* to it, and also that the totality in question is, at the same time, *overdetermined* by totalities of a higher complexity . . .) and *thirdly*, the *historical relativity* of all totality, namely that the totality-character of all totality is changing, disintegrating, confined to a determinate, concrete historical period."[36] The significance and limits of an action, measure, achievement, law, etc., cannot be therefore assessed except in relation to a dialectical grasp of the structure of totality. This in turn necessarily implies the task of a dialectical grasp of the complex mediations which constitute the structure of totality.

The early Lukács was unable to formulate the concept of "concrete totality" because he was not in a position to envisage those mediations which could transcend the "details, fragments, isolated things" of the "immediately given" in the ultimate unity of a dynamically changing dialectical totality. The picture of an unmediated, segmented, non-interconnected, statically frozen conglomeration of discrete things could only generate an equally static concept of totality: a nostalgic value-postulate of unity. By the time of writing *History and Class-Consciousness* the vision has changed qualitatively. Discussing the problem of "ultimate aim" (*Endziel*) Lukács writes:

It is also no *ought*, no *idea*, which would be associated with the "real" process in a regulative way.

Rather, the ultimate aim is the *relation to the whole* (to the whole of society, regarded as a process), through which every individual moment of the struggle first receives its revolutionary significance. It is a relation which *dwells within* every moment in its simple and sober everydayness, but which first *becomes real through its becoming conscious,* and which (by *making manifest the relation to the whole*) gives reality to the moment of daily struggle, *raising it to reality* out of *mere factuality,* mere existence.[37]

The problematic aspects of Lukács' conception of "Subject-Object-relations", characteristic of this period of his development, can be detected in this passage. But also it can be clearly seen that this concept of totality is already a dynamically mediated one, though of course it cannot go beyond the limitations imposed on Lukács by the lack of a greater concreteness in his conception of "mediation" at the time.

In Lukács' development the concept of "mediation" has been taken up over and over again. The fight against the meaninglessness of "immediacy" (*Unmittelbarkeit*) is characteristic of Lukács' approach right from the beginning: one cannot fail to see this in *The Soul and the Forms* and in *Aesthetic Culture*— not to speak of *The Theory of the Novel.* "Aestheticism", "naturalism", "impressionistic description", etc., are rejected by him because of their fragmented character: their inability to produce the picture of a coherent whole. At the same time "symbolism" is also rejected, because the picture it produces is that of an artificial, false, abstract-subjective totality, in so far as the immediacy of detail is directly—and with subjective arbitrariness—elevated to the status of universal significance, comprehensiveness. (The earlier quoted passage concerning Thomas Mann's irony is revealing also in this respect.) The common denominator between "naturalism" and "symbolism" is, of course, the missing mediation, and thus their close interrelatedness, despite their superficial contrasts at various levels—subject-matter, linguistic characterization, external form, etc.—is understood, even if at this stage only as a hunch, rather than a coherently developed insight. The young Lukács does not possess the conceptual apparatus that would enable him to transform that hunch into a systematic theoretical vision. The abstractness of his own general level of inquiry—the categories of "the soul and the forms" (*die Seele und die Formen*), "value and reality" (*Wert und Wirklichkeit*), "the height of being" (*Gipfel des Seins*), "appearance and essence" (*Schein und Wesen*), "life and work of art" (*Leben und Kunstwerk*), "pure constraint on the pure will" (*der reine Zwang auf den reinen Willen*), "the pinnacle of being" (*der Hohepunkt des Daseins*), etc. etc.—prevented him from identifying those concrete mediations which could transcend the rejected immediacy by moving towards a concrete totality, and not towards some abstract

"metaphysical essence", as happens in the early works.
The contradiction between grasping the meaninglessness of immediacy and Lukács' inability to solve con-
ceptually the complex problems involved in the dialectical relationship between mediation and totality
results in a false conception of the critic's role:

> "The critic is the man who sees what is fateful in the
> forms, whose strongest *experience* is that *spiritual
> content* which the forms conceal within themselves,
> *indirectly* and unconsciously." "The essay is a court,
> but what is essential and value-determining in it is
> not the *judgement* (as in the case of the *system*), but
> the *process of judging*."[38]

Thus the elements of truth are pushed to the point of
mysticism, in order to hide, however unconsciously,
the ultimate contradiction that what is being opposed
to the fragmented immediacy of "naturalism", "symbolism", etc.—by means of the categorial apparatus
of *The Soul and the Forms*, etc.—is a mystical immediacy of frozen metaphysical essences. If one starts
—as Lukács does—from the premise that philosophy
can offer the "icy finality of perfection",[39] the margin
of the critic's activity is an illusory one. The "process"
he opposes to the "icy finality of perfection" as displayed in philosophy is "predetermined" by those
metaphysical "soul-contents" which the critic is supposed to "strongly experience", "directly live", and
thus to free from that "mediatedness", and "uncons-

cious hiddenness" which inevitably characterize them as they assume the forms of "sensible immediacy" (*sinnliche Unmittelbarkeit*). The critic is given the task of opposing the "soulless immediacy" of naturalism, etc., as well as indicating those forms of "sensible immediacy" which are penetrated by "soul-contents", i.e. in which a "metaphysical immediacy" takes on a directly perceptible form. But in the end there is no criterion of judgment, neither for the rejected immediacy nor for the romanticized one. This is why the "process of judging" must be mystified *per se* and opposed to the "judgment" characteristic of the "system". The critic's role as an intermediary between the "forms" and the "system" is an illusory one, for the metaphysical entities of the "system" are taken for granted and are assigned the metaphysical value-quotient of the "finality of perfection". The problem of mediation, despite the recognition of the "bad immediacy" of naturalism, symbolism, etc., remains unresolved. And this is what defeats the young Lukács in the end, forcing him to search for a solution where it cannot be found : in a mystically inclined opposition to "the system".

But even if the young Lukács failed to master the problem of concrete totality through the grasp of the concrete mediations that constitute it, one should not underestimate the fact that the negative side of the issue—in the form of the repeated polemics against the immediacy of aestheticism, impressionism, naturalism, symbolism, etc.—is tackled with great rigour and sensitivity. We can recognize here, in fact, a major theme of Lukács' later aesthetic writings : the analysis of the profound structural affinity between naturalism and symbolism as regards their inability adequately to transcend the level of crude immediacy. The paradoxical phenomenon of naturalism verging on symbolism, or even turning into symbolism, on the one hand, and symbolism falling back on naturalistic positions on the other finds its explanation in the structural affinity of missing mediations. Clear definitions in this regard can only be found in the later Lukács, but this complex of problems has been inherited from the author of *The Soul and the Forms*.

The road towards greater concreteness as regards the concrete mediations of concrete totality led through the earlier mentioned crisis in the years 1914-17. What is significant in this context is that in this period the earlier unquestioned "system" is submitted to searching examination and is found hopelessly wanting, so much so in fact that it had to be abandoned. Thus the "icy finality of perfection" at a closer look turned out to be the lifeless perfection of a frozen dialectic : the transformation of the categories of an originally dialectical quest for the transcendence of immediacy into the frozen essences of a metaphysical immediacy. No wonder that the "six-legged monster" could not be brought to an organic conclusion : every new attempt at remedying its defects could only add a new frozen member, thus underlining the contradictions of the conception as a whole. And the help Lukács could receive from the Hegelian philosophy was here of no use whatsoever. For, as he later realized, Hegel tried to tackle this complex of problems:

> . . . as purely theoretical, as logical. . . . As a result, the *mediating categories achieved independence* as real "essences"; they freed themselves from the *real historical* process, from the basis of their genuine comprehensibility, and so turned into a *petrified new immediacy.*[40]

A system of this kind could be of no help, except in an indirect way, i.e. by displaying the contradictions of such an approach. Lukács himself had to abandon first the premises of his earlier system before he could find a satisfactory solution to the problem of immediacy-mediations-totality. His encounter with Marxism brought home to him the fact that the crucial intermediary link of all human phenomena is man's "practico-critical activity", with its ultimate reference—a reference "in the last analysis"—to the sphere of economics. His reckoning with the Hegelian philosophy in *History and Class-Consciousness*— especially in its central piece on *Reification and the Consciousness of the Proletariat*—is unequivocal and conclusive in this respect. It forcefully makes the point that the Marxist critique of political economy is methodologically based on the Hegelian programme

of the "dissolution of immediacy" which for Hegel
had to remain an abstract and unrealizable programme, because of the socio-historical limitations of
his standpoint. At the same time it is repeatedly
stressed that the crux of the matter is the complexity
of "concrete mediations" : if the latter are suppressed,
the result is inevitably something negative, or even
dangerous, like "vulgar Marxism", "economism",
"ethical utopianism", *"Proletkult"*, "sectarianism",
"schematism", "naturalism", "revolutionary romanticism" (a version of "symbolism"), "voluntarism",
"subjectivism", "Stalinism", etc. etc. What is common, according to Lukács, to all these trends and
manifestations is the neglect or suppression of the
categories of mediation.

Thus in Lukács' conception the role of economics,
far from being mechanical and one-sidedly determ-
inistic, is dialectically active : it is given the role of
the structurally and methodologically ultimate frame
of reference. This does not mean, of course, that now
we have acquired a "magic wand" in the shape of a
mechanical "common denominator". On the contrary, the assertion about the importance of economics
becomes meaningful only if one is able to grasp the
manifold specific mediations in the most varied fields
of human activity, which are not simply "built upon"
an "economic reality" but also actively structure the
latter through the immensely complex and relatively
autonomous structure of their own. Only if one grasps

dialectically the multiplicity of specific mediations can one understand the Marxian notion of economics. For if the latter is the "ultimate determinant", it is also a "determined determinant" : it does not exist outside the always concrete, historically changing complex of concrete mediations, including the most "spiritual" ones. If the "demystification" of capitalist society, because of the fetish-character of its mode of production and exchange, has to start from the analysis of economics, this does not mean in the least that the results of such economic inquiry can be simply transferred to other spheres and levels. Even as regards the culture, politics, law, religion, art, ethics, etc., of capitalist society one has still to find those complex mediations, at various levels of historico-philosophical generalization, which enable one to reach reliable conclusions both about the specific ideological form in question and about the given, historically concrete form of capitalistic society as a whole. And this is more evident if one tries to transfer the inquiry to a more general level, as becomes in fact necessary in the course of the structural analysis of any particular form of society, or of any specific form of human activity. One cannot grasp the "specific" without identifying its manifold interconnections with a given system of complex mediations. In other words : one must be able to see the "atemporal" (systematic) elements in temporality, and the temporal elements in the systematic factors. It is in relation to this point that Lukács stresses the fundamental differences between Marx and Hegel, while emphasizing the great achievements of the latter:

Hegel's tremendous intellectual contribution consisted in the fact that he made *theory* and *history* *dialectically relative* to each other, grasped them in a dialectical reciprocal penetration. Ultimately, however, his attempt was a failure. He could never get as far as the *genuine unity of theory and practice*; all that he could do was either fill the logical sequence of the categories with rich historical material, or rationalize history, in the shape of a succession of forms, structural changes, epochs, etc., which he raised to the level of categories by sublimating and abstracting them. Marx was the first who was able to see through this false dilemma. He did not derive the *succession of categories* either from their *logical sequence*, or from their *historical succession*, but recognized "their succession as determined through the relation which they have to each other in bourgeois society". In this way, he did not merely give dialectic the real basis which Hegel sought in vain, he did not merely put it on its feet, but he also raised the critique of political economy (which he had made the basis of dialectics) out of the fetishistic rigidity and abstractive narrowness to which economics was subject, even in the case of its greatest bourgeois representatives. The critique of political economy is no longer one science along with others, is not merely set over the others as a "basic science"; rather, it *embraces the whole world of history* of the "forms of existence" (the categories) of human society.[41]

73

This conception of economics as the dialectical comprehension of all the categories of human society, through their complex transformations in history, could not be further away from a mechanistic vision. For the immense variety of categories can be interrelated in a coherent whole only if the "model" of general assessment is that of multiple transitions and mediations, qualified both historically and systematically.

Lukács' philosophical achievements reach as far as his conception of mediation (totality) allows him to go. It goes without saying, however, that his conception has been profoundly affected by his historical predicament as a critic, politician and philosopher. The issue of mediation is not just one among many, nor is it simply an abstract philosophical problem, however complex and "abstract" many of its aspects might be. When Lukács strongly criticizes Feuerbach's "ethical utopianism"[42] as the result of a myopic rejection of the Hegelian category of "mediation", he is also fighting a battle against a utopian trend in the existing socialist movement. Similarly his criticism of "vulgar Marxism", "economism", "sectarianism", "naturalism", "*Proletkult*", "schematism", "revolutionary romanticism", "Zhdanovism", "voluntarism", "subjectivism", "Stalinism", etc., has always a mark of historical urgency, just as much as his polemics directed against the other side, against "irrationalism", "decadentism", "the myth of immediacy", etc. etc.

Lukács lives and works at a time when "the mystifications of capitalistic immediacy" have already penetrated the organized socialist movement ("economism", "revisionism", etc.), and when the society that emerged after the victorious October Revolution is being conditioned and affected in more ways than one by the "irrational" moves of this system of "reified immediacies". The theoretical task is seen as a challenge of great practical significance. This is how Lukács assesses, for instance, the sectarian approach:

> The sectarian world-view which politically underrates the *mediatory role* of the *immediate interests* (incentives) in the realization of world historical tasks creates the same kind of dogmatism at the level of the individual's conception of the world: a dogmatism that dismisses all the mediatory factors.[43]

It is obvious enough that the issue is not an academic one, for the dismissal of "all the mediatory factors" is not far from the tragedy of the concentration camps. In *History and Class-Consciousness, Moses Hess, The Young Hegel, Essays on Realism, The Category of Besonderheit, Die Eigenart des Ästhetischen,* we observe Lukács' theoretical quest for a deeper understanding of the complexities of mediation in a world dominated by the dangerously narrow perspectives that arise on the foundations of reifying immediacies. The quest acquires its practical pathos in this context: as a philosopher's answer to an historical challenge. And no matter what one might think of some parts of *The Destruction of Reason*, its really fine and gripping chapters acquire their significance in the same context.

Lukács' achievements are outstanding in those of his works in which the inquiry can legitimately remain at a more abstract level. In such works he systematically explores the intricate problems of mediation under its manifold aspects as no philosopher before or beside him. The outcome is not only the solution of numerous complex aesthetic issues, but also the formulation of some fundamental and challenging problems in the fields of Epistemology, Ethics, Ontology and Philosophy of History.

However, the general theoretical nature of his conception of mediation proves to be a self-imposed trap in certain situations; namely in circumstances in which even a simple inventory of the socio-historical ingredients at work would reveal much more than Lukács' far-fetched and completely unrealistic theoretical assessment of the presumed new historical trends. As an example, let us quote his discussion of the characteristics of the "new democracy", i.e. of the "People's Democracy":

The true democracy—the new democracy—produces everywhere real, *dialectical transitions* between private and public life. The turning point in the new democracy is that now man participates in the interactions of private and public life as an *active subject*

76

and not as a *passive object*. . . . The ethically emerging new phase demonstrates above all that one man's freedom is not a hindrance to another's freedom but its precondition. The individual cannot be really free except in a free society. . . . The now emerging self-consciousness of mankind announces as a perspective the end of human "prehistory". With this, man's self-creation acquires a new accent; now as a trend we see the emergence of a unity between the individual's human self-constitution and the self-creation of mankind. *Ethics is a crucial intermediary link in this whole process.*[44]

As we can see, this analysis is hopelessly off-target as a concrete assessment of a particular historical situation : it is, in fact, a succession of general philosophical postulates represented as actually existing social trends. In this it strongly resembles the earlier quoted passage, written at the beginning of 1919, on the occasion of the unification of the two Hungarian workers' Parties (see p. 54): the same approach, the same attempt at directly linking—without the necessary "mediations"—a particular historical situation with far-away "world-historical perspectives". We are confronted here with philosophico-moral anticipations, with the reassertion of the validity of some fundamental moral postulates, with an invitation to realize some basic tenets of the Marxist programme—in a situation in which the political power-requirements of translating a programme into reality seem to be satisfied—but not with a realistic grasp of the specific features and contradictions of a social formation.

The unreality of the 1919 analysis might have been explained as due to Lukács' political inexperience, although—as we have seen—even then things were much more complex than that. Almost thirty years later, at the time of writing about "the new democracy", the hypothesis of political inexperience is definitely a non-starter. After all, in the meantime Lukács lived through not only the dramatic months of the Hungarian Soviet Republic, followed by the long years of political emigration both in the west and in Moscow, but also he had to experience personally the political prisons of the Stalinist system. If despite all this he nourishes the illusions we have just seen, this cannot be explained with a tautological reference to the illusions themselves. Rather : an explanation ought to be attempted in terms of the philosopher's life and its interactions with the system of his ideas.

As has already been mentioned, the limits of Lukács' philosophical achievements are set by his own conception of mediation or, to be more precise, by the defects of this conception : by the unwarranted intrusion of "immediacy" into his general world-view. This can be clearly seen in both the 1919 and the 1947 quotations in the direct transference of a particular social pattern to a most general world-historical level. This, however, in itself is no explanation. The question that

needs answering is : why does such undialectical transference occur in some specific connections of Lukács'
thought, despite his unrivalled general awareness of
the crucial importance of mediations?

To find an answer to this question one must try to
understand the abstract character of the political
dimension of his conception of mediation. The major
determinants in this respect cannot be confined to
the already mentioned socio-political immobility that
dominated the years of Lukács' intellectual formation
in his native country. Nor could they be exhausted
with a reference to the rarefied atmosphere of politics
in a weak emigration (i.e. in a political emigration
devoid of a broadly based social support in its country
of origin) in which Lukács tried to overcome the handicaps of his beginnings. The *"übergreifendes Moment"*
(overriding factor) was the fundamental change in the
organized international socialist movement in the
twenties, following the changes in Soviet internal
development as a result of Stalin's victory. Parallel
with these developments the political trend represented
by Lukács within the Hungarian Party was defeated
by the end of the twenties, and with the defeat of his
so-called *"Blum-theses"*—in 1928—he ceased to play
any significant political role. (Even during the post-
war years of the "new democracy", before he was
attacked by Révai and others for his "deviations", his
role was strictly confined to the politically subordin-
ated realm of culture. He was not allowed in the

large body of the Central Committee, let alone given
a place in the effective organ of political direction, the
Politbüro.) His *History and Class-Consciousness* was
strongly attacked, by Comintern officials and others,
and later too attacks and intrigues continued to restrict
his range of action even before the final blow of the
defeat of his "Blum-theses". These are the personal
aspects of his political non-evolution. More important
were, however, the general trends of development,
quite independently of their personal repercussions
which in the philosopher's mind could have been
ascribed to the excesses of narrow-minded party functionaries. We can single out here only one aspect of this
development : the practical disintegration of all forms
of effective political mediation, from the Workers'
Councils to the Trade Unions. Even the Party, in the
course of its adaptation to the requirements of Stalinistic policies, had largely lost its mediatory function
and potential. If Lukács' idea of the Party as formulated in *History and Class-Consciousness* contained a
great deal of idealization, in the changed circumstances this idealization has become overwhelming.
All the more because in *History and Class-Consciousness* the institution of the Workers' Councils still
appeared as a necessary form of mediation and its
effective instrumentality. Now, however, its place had
to be left empty, as indeed all the other forms of
political mediation too had to leave a vacuum behind
them. In this respect the twenties not only did not

bring a political evolution but unmistakably marked a phase of involution in political realism.

This is where one can see the contradictions between the limited immediacy of political perspectives and the universality of a socialist programme in Lukács' conception. Since the political intermediaries—and instrumental guarantees—are missing, the gap between the immediacy of socio-political realities and the general programme of Marxism has to be filled by means of assigning the role of mediation to ethics, by declaring that "ethics is a crucial intermediary link in this whole process". Thus the absence of effective mediatory forces is "remedied" by a direct appeal to "reason", to man's "moral responsibility", to the "moral pathos of life", to the "responsibility of the intellectuals", etc. etc. So that—paradoxical as it might seem—Lukács finds himself in this respect in the position of "ethical utopianism", despite his repeated polemics against it, and despite his clear realization that the intellectual roots of ethical utopianism can be pinpointed in the lack of mediations. (Lukács' significant overrating of the role of the intellectuals in contemporary society belongs to the same complex of problems.)

The direct extrapolation from the prevailing form of unmediated instrumentality to the universal perspectives of socialism, and vice versa, confers a certain abstractness on more than one of Lukács' analyses. And no wonder. For the "concrete mediations" that constitute "concrete totality" are closely interrelated (and reciprocally interpenetrating) partial totalities; they acquire the character of a totality from the reciprocal interpenetration of the various modalities and forms of mediation. Thus the abstractness of the political dimension in one's conception of this dialectical system of mediations leaves its marks, though of course not in the same way and degree, on the various complexes of problems, whether in Aesthetics or in Ontology, in Epistemology or indeed in Ethics itself to which that problematical role of "should-be mediation" is assigned. (It is not difficult to see, to take only one example, that in order to be able to fulfil its "mediatory function" Ethics needs the support of the very instruments and effective forces of mediation which it is supposed to replace in Lukács' conception.)

Similarly, it is rather inconsistent of Lukács that, while he condemns Zhdanovism and its "unmediated" theory of "revolutionary romanticism", he accepts the narrow and unmediated instrumentality that necessarily produces it. His analyses of this cultural-ideological phenomenon remain inevitably abstract in the sense that the concrete social determinants of Zhdanovism cannot be revealed. The discourse is confined to the ideological sphere, and at times the actual causal relations are even reversed: it appears as if the aberrations and contradictions of the ideological level were responsible for the ills of social development and therefore the remedies should be found at that level, by means of an intense ideological clarification. (Of course they were also responsible for those ills; but basically they were determined by them, they were specific manifestations of them.) "Sectarianism" represented a similar issue. Here too Lukács' correct recognition and penetrating dialectical analysis of the missing mediations in the sectarian approach could not alter in the least the fact that sectarianism as an ideological form was determined by the actual absence of effective mediatory forces and institutions from the social body: it reflected this state of affairs, it did not cause it. (Of course it also contributed to the solidification and perpetuation of the social structures which necessarily brought it into being.) To envisage remedies simply by means of an ideological clarification, however rigorous, against this background of social determinations reminds one of the attempts directed at disposing of religious alienation by means of noble atheistic sermons.

The actual absence of socio-political mediatory forces and institutions in Soviet development greatly affected Lukács' perspectives, undermining the possibility of practical-political criticism: from the end of the twenties, criticism was condemned to become abstract-theoretical and generic-ideological. (Its practical side was narrowly circumscribed by the only feasible instrumentality: the Stalinist Party as the final arbiter over the fate of the competing ideological positions.) To make things worse, Soviet society had become internationally isolated and confronted with extreme hostility by the incomparably more powerful capitalist world. In these circumstances it became ever more difficult to envisage concrete material forces of socio-political mediation as an effective form of practical criticism of the prevailing trend of Stalinism. Soviet development thus increasingly acquired the character of a "model" of socialism, despite the obvious violations of some elementary principles of socialism, however paradoxical this might seem. Its complete international isolation—which in fact greatly contributed to the weakening and ultimate disintegration of the internal forces of mediation and thus to the bureaucratic violations of socialist principles—restricted the margin of action of all those who in an ever more polarized world (one should not forget the dramatic rise of European Fascism) refused to turn against the only existing social system that professed socialist principles and *de facto* became the "model", however paradoxical and problematic, of socialism. In this restricted field of action their discourse—in the absence of both external and internal mediatory and conditioning forces of a socialist character—was confined to the ideological sphere. Since the historically conditioned narrow instrumentality of Soviet developments had to be directly linked with the universal perspectives of socialism in the idea of "Socialism in one country", the general moral perspective itself had to be turned into a mediatory force. Needless to say this could be done only at the level of theoretical abstraction. This is why in the end *"der Zwiespalt von Sein und Sollen ist nicht aufgehoben"*, for the philosophically postulated mediatory force, in order to become reality, would itself need actual, effective mediatory forces and instruments. An anticipated moral postulate, as mediator between the ultimate postulates of the universal perspectives of socialism and the immediacy of a given situation, is and necessarily remains a pseudo-mediator, an ideological postulate, an ultimate *"Sollen"*. And to mediate between *"Sein und Sollen"* by means of another *"Sollen"* amounts to not mediating at all. For the *"Zwiespalt von Sein und Sollen"* cannot be superseded through postulating another *"Sollen"* which is then projected and superimposed on the immediate reality of "the new democracy", for instance. The numerous unfulfilled optimistic anticipations of Lukács' writings—later recognized as unfulfilled by the philosopher himself—find their explanation in this contradiction inherent in his position and thought.

Needless to say, the "ought-ridden" character of Lukács' solution is not simply the manifestation of personal limitations. The basic determinants are those of the concrete historical situation which set the ultimate limits to any personal achievement. Lukács' significance consists in his ability to explore the objectively given field of action to its extreme limits, creating thus a life-work simply incommensurable with philosophical achievements produced within the Soviet world. Paradoxically, in this the same "*Sollen*" that circumscribed the limits of his achievements proved to be his greatest asset. For he never accepted the immediately given in its crude immediacy, i.e. he never abandoned for a moment the ultimate perspectives of socialism. As was mentioned earlier, his perspectives were characterized by a duality, in the form of linking the everyday issues with the broadest general aims of a socialist mankind. In this duality of perspectives the dominating factor always remained the incessant advocacy—however "ought-ridden"—of the ultimate socialist goals and values. Though this has given an abstract character to so many of his analyses, it also enabled him to keep alive, with the greatest intellectual rigour, socialist ideals and use them as a general framework of criticism of the immediately given. True, this criticism always remained confined to the ideological sphere—even after the officially-announced programme of "destalinization". But in the latter he achieved more than anybody else, thanks to the validity of his "ought-ridden" ultimate postulates and perspectives.

If the contradictions of Lukács' position now appear to be obvious, this is because the historical perspectives themselves have significantly changed. To what extent Lukács can keep pace with such change, remains to be seen. (That he made great efforts to do so, both in his *Aesthetics* and in his *Social Ontology*, is clear enough, however problematic the results might be.) What matters in this connection is that his old perspectives, personally and historically valid in the sense which has been shown, now irrevocably belong to the past. There is no room here for an adequate discussion of these problems. It must be stressed, however, that the question of the "mediation of socialism with socialism" has ceased to be an abstract moral postulate and has become an often rather confusing, disconcerting and even disorienting reality. We are faced today with objective tensions and contradictions within the socialist world. The issues that have thus arisen cannot even be tackled, let alone solved, with ideological labels like "sectarianism" which Lukács tried to stick, in one of his recent essays, on to the body of Chinese development. Some fundamental reassessments would be required in the present situation; all the more because another new, and perhaps the most important, historical factor—the profound structural crisis of the most advanced capitalistic countries and the potential new social dynamism closely connected with it—raises the question of socialism in a radically different way. It seems, however, that Lukács is unable to reformulate the question of mediation as an institutionally safeguarded internal necessity of socialism, because this would imply the presence of objective contradictions within and between socialist systems: a sharp contrast to his advocacy of "Reason" and "ideological clarification" as a solution to the existing problems. On the other hand, he seems to be too ready to accept the prospects of "many decades" of social stagnation and immobility in developed capitalist countries, naïvely expecting a "turn towards socialism" in these countries as a result of the "force of attraction" of Soviet-type socialism that succeeded in freeing itself "from the remnants of Stalinism". Thus the solutions are, again, confined to the ideological sphere.

The total unreality of Lukács' position is graphically displayed in a context where he praises the Kennedy-type "Brains-Trust as an organizational form" as valid also for socialism. His words are as follows:

> A Kennedy knew for certain that he was no theoretician and no man of science, but (in contrast with European, and specifically with German development) he did not identify the expert with the top-level bureaucrat. He knew that from *this* expert he could discover nothing of importance, but that what he needed was a set of intellectuals and theoreticians. (Whether or not Kennedy chose correctly, is unimportant here.) These theoreticians were to do nothing but devote their knowledge and their thought to the exposure of general problems, so that the politician could derive from this material the slogans for his movement. Now, I believe that the specific position of Marx and Lenin in socialist countries has led to a fantastic over-estimation of the theoretical value of the Party's First Secretary.

With the Brains-Trust, "a new organizational

principle has appeared, namely, a *duality* and a co-activity of theory and political practice, which is no longer unified in one person—and which happened to be unified only once, if at all—but which, on account of the extraordinary widening of the tasks, *can be brought about today only in such a dual form.*"[45]

It is pathetic to see this great demystifier of our century yielding to sheer mystification. Almost every single element of this assessment is hopelessly out of touch with reality. George Kennan, perhaps the best brain of Kennedy's Brains-Trust, has a much lower opinion of this "organizational form". He knows that its actual working principle is: "Leave your brains and ideals behind you when you enter this Brains-Trust", that is if your ideals happen to differ from those of the "top-level bureaucrats" ("*hohen Büro-kraten*"). (He wrote after his resignation from the Kennedy team that the only occasion when those bureacrats could not prevail over him was when he donated his blood after the Skopje earthquake: they could not prevent *that* from happening.) Also, the issue is not whether we abound in men of the stature of a Marx or a Lenin. (Though again significantly the names of both Gramsci and Mao Tse-tung are omitted.) The rarity of intellectually creative political talent is not some "original cause", but rather the *effect* of a certain type of social development, which not only prevents the emergence of new talent, but

destroys the talent available through political trials
(cf. the numerous Russian intellectuals and politicians
liquidated in the thirties), through the expulsion of
men of talent from the field of politics (Lukács, for
instance), or through bending them to the acceptance
of the narrow practical perspectives of the given situation (e.g. the great talent, by the highest standards, of
a József Révai). Lukács himself was denounced as a
"professor" when he tried to integrate politics and
theory,[46] and he had to leave the field of politics as
a result of successive attacks. He accepted this turn
of events with resignation. Now, however, he invents
a theory to justify the permanent "duality" and separation of theory and politics: the "widening of the
tasks" ("*Verbreitung der Aufgaben*"). The earlier
resignation now becomes a mystified virtue through
the assertion of its alleged necessity. "*Der Zwiespalt
von Sein und Sollen ist nicht aufgehoben*", it merely
seems to be. For the advocated "organizational form"
as the synthesis between theory and practice only
appears to be a practical reality; it is in fact a mere
utopian postulate. It is no more than a pious hope to
expect the frustrated Kennan's bureaucrats to give
way to his insights and proposals, just as much as it is
a mere wishful thinking to expect the solution of the
great structural problems of international socialism
to come from the self-conscious and willing recognition by Party First Secretaries that they are neither
Marxes nor Lenins. If it is true, as it well may be,

that we are today confronted with an "extraordinary widening of tasks" ("*ausserordentliche Verbreitung der Aufgaben*"), this makes it all the more urgent and vital to insist on the reciprocal interpenetration of theory and politics, theory and practice, rather than to offer a justification of their alienation and "necessary duality" by idealizing an organizational form, a non-existent or unworkable "Brains Trust". Nothing could be more illusory than to expect the solution of our problems from the "Brains-Trust" of abstract intellectuals and narrowly pragmatic politicians. The alleged "*Verbreitung der Aufgaben*" needs for its solution the reciprocal interpenetration of theory and practice in all spheres of human activity and at all levels, from the lowest to the highest, and not the sterile stalemate of academics and politicians at the top. In other words the task is a radical democratization and restructuring of all social structures and not the utopian reassembly of existing hierarchies.

7. Conclusion

As we have seen, the thread of an unresolved duality leads, in one form or in another, through Lukács entire development. We have also seen the close connection between the structure of his ideas and some fundamental trends of development of an age of which Lukács is one of the greatest representatives. If we are reluctant today to accept some basic tenets of his social ontology, this is not because of some sudden conceptual inspiration, but because we feel its inadequacies as regards the possibility of answers to our practical problems. Reluctant to accept the "many decades" of social immobility he prophesies, we are forced to question the elements of dualism in his social ontology. This we must do with great caution; not only because his systematic work on Social Ontology still awaits publication and the samples from it, contained in his *Gespräche*, are inevitably summary and schematic, but also because the animating element of our own questioning is a hope, not a certainty. The emerging new historical perspectives seem to sustain this hope, but they do not warrant its transformation into a self-reassuring certainty. Lukács' notion of a *"rein objektive Entwicklung der Arbeit"* (*purely objective* development of labour) that necessarily produces *"ein immer kleineres Minimum der Arbeit"* (an ever-diminishing minimum of necessary labour) seems to us rather problematical. It does not raise, in the first place, the question of the *limits* of such *"rein objektive Entwicklung"*, granted that we accept this notion as an element of ontological discussion. (The question of limits is a vitally important one; its absence creates a wide gap that can only be filled by trust. E.g. *"La vérité est en marche"*, etc.) Secondly, by postulating a *"rein objektive Entwicklung"* within a *dual* causality, we are pushing things to their extreme poles, in order to find an "ontological place" for the recommended mediatory function of Ethics. In fact an answer to the question of limits might yield a unified and integrate system of causality which would fill the "ontological gap" reserved by Lukács for his *"Sollen"* ("ought"), for the never ceasing moral appeals of his thought.

At the same time it ought to be stressed that though the general historical perspectives have changed, the socio-political trends that form the basis of many of

Lukács' formulations are still very much alive today and are being transformed only in the dialectical sense of "continuity in discontinuity". Thus his discourse concerning the undialectical "immediacies" of various ideological trends retains its general methodological validity, and at times even its urgent topicality, in the relevant ideological sphere. Also it should not be forgotten that the dilemmas Lukács had to face in his efforts at defining his position in relation to Marx's postulate of the unity of Philosophy and Politics, Theory and Practice, were not simply personal dilemmas but representative of a difficult age in which the given problematical perspectives seemed to prevail for a long time over the historical orientation of the socialist movement. Opinions may differ as to the practical validity of some of Lukács' conclusions. But no one should fail to see the representative monumentality of his undertaking.

NOTES

1. *Gespräche mit Georg Lukács.* Rowohlt, Hamburg, 1967, p. 109. Unless mention is made to the contrary, translations from the German in this paper are the work of G. H. R. Parkinson, to whom grateful acknowledgement is made. Translations from the Hungarian are my own. This essay, written in 1967/8, first appeared in a volume edited by Dr. Parkinson.

2. *"Postscriptum 1957 zu: Mein Weg zu Marx."* In: *Georg Lukács: Schriften zur Ideologie und Politik.* Lutcherhand, Neuwied and Berlin, 1967, p. 657.

3. Quoted by Thomas Mann in his *Essay in Autobiography.*

4. Although many of Lukács' works deal with German topics, and although his attachment to German culture—in particular to the German philosophical heritage—is really very profound, his writings on German problems are unmistakably those of an "outsider". In fact his work as a whole cannot be understood without the Hungarian cultural and historical setting that greatly affected not only his early development but also, in more ways than one, his later orientation.

5. *"Új magyar lira."* (New Hungarian Lyric Poetry) In: *Huszadik Század* (Twentieth Century) Vol. 2 (1909) pp. 286-92 and 419-24.

6. *"Ady, a magyar tragédía nagy énekese."* (Ady, Great Poet of the Hungarian Tragedy) 1939, p. 28 of the volume *Az Irástudók Felelössége* (The Intellectuals' Responsibility), Moscow, 1944.

7. See pp. 62-4 of this essay, on Lukács' conception of the complex causality at work in the structure of totality.

8. A group of intellectuals used to meet regularly on Sundays in a private circle, until it was broken up by the upheav⸱ at the end of the war. The undisputed intellectual he ⸺ of this circle was Lukács, and several of its members later acquired world fame. To name but a few: Frigyes Antal, Béla Balazs, Béla Fogarasi, Arnold Hauser, Zoltán Kodály, Karl Mannheim, Wilhelm Szilasi, Charles de Tolnay, Eugene Varga, John Wilde.

9. "Esztétikai Kultúra." (Aesthetic Culture) In: *Renaissance, 1910.*

10. "Az erkölcs szerepe a komunista termelésben." (The Role of Morality in Communist Production.) Reproduced in the volume cited in Note 2. The quotation is from pp. 79-80 of this volume.

11. At the beginning of this essay (cf. pp.14-5) we quoted a passage written in 1957, in which Lukács expressed his faith in the positive solution of the problems of the socialist movement. The same faith is expressed, in almost identical terms, thirty-eight years earlier when he writes at the end of "The Role of Morality in Communist Production":

> It is impossible for the proletariat, which has hitherto remained true to its world-historical vocation under much more difficult conditions, to abandon this vocation at the very moment that it is finally in a position to realize it in action. Op. cit., p. 81.

12. In 1919, when Horthy's men pressed the Austrian Government to extradite Lukács, a group of intellectuals published an appeal to save him:

> He had given up the seductions of the pampered life which was his inheritance, in favour of the position of

responsible solitary thought. When he turned to politics he sacrificed what was dearest to him, his freedom of thought, to the reformer's work which he intended to fulfil . . . Saving Lukács is no party matter. It is the duty of all who have personal experience of his *human purity,* and of the many who admire the lofty-minded intellectuality of his philosophical and aesthetic works, to protest against the extradition.

In *Berliner Tageblatt,* 12 November 1919. Signed by Franz Ferdinand Baumgarten, Richard Beer-Hoffmann, Richard Dehmel, Paul Ernst, Bruno Frank, Maximilian Harden, Alfred Kerr, Heinrich Mann, Thomas Mann, Emil Praetorius, Karl Scheffler.

13. *Geschichte und Klassenbewusstsein.* Malik Verlag, Berlin, 1923, p. 54. Lukács' later formulated "partisan-strategy" is still well within the limits of the same conception of an institutional framework. By contrast, Gramsci's idea of the "hegemony of the proletariat" is a qualitatively different concept.

14. Lukács' assessment of the Chinese situation is extremely problematical. It is based on the false premise that the destiny of mankind will be decided by the greater ideological "force of attraction" (*Anziehungskraft*) of one of the "*two* systems". Both elements of this premise are unrealistic. The idea of an ideological "*Anziehungskraft*" minimizes the role of objective internal contradictions. (This problem will be discussed in section 6 of the present essay.) If however the institutional framework of one of the "two systems" is taken for granted, there remains no room for criticism except appeals concerning the possible improvement of the ideological "force of attraction" of Soviet-type socialism. More important is, however, the assumption according to which "two systems" are involved in the "*internationalen Klassenkampf der Koexistenz*" (international class-struggle of co-existence). In reality the military stalemate that forces "co-existence" on the two political-military power blocs sets free the development

of a multiplicity of transitional systems, with internal dynamisms—and contradictions—as well as objective interests of their own. Consequently it is impossible to reduce this complexity to the scheme of "two systems". The artificial unity of "two power blocs" (in the past corresponding, in fact, to two systems), viewed at the social level, belongs irrevocably to the past. No amount of "ideological clarification and persuasion" can explain way the objective differences of interest and of internal dynamism that involve even the sharpest oppositions among the multiplicity of transitional systems. This historical change requires a much more complex strategic assessment of the trends of socialist transformation and rules out the acceptance of Lukács' model of the "ideological force of attraction" of Soviet-type socialism. At the same time it must be stressed that no matter how problematical Lukács' approach to the Chinese problem may be, the duality of his perspectives enables him to raise some fundamental theoretical issues connected with the dialectical category of "mediation". Irrespective of the concrete historical framework to which he applies his theoretical considerations—the contemporary Chinese situation —his reflection on the inherent relationship between "sectarianism" and "lack of mediations" has a general methodological validity in its applications to the ideological sphere. (See his essay: "Zur Debatte zwischen China und der Sovjet-union. Theoretisch-philosophische Bemerkungen." In: *Georg Lukács: Schriften zur Ideologie und Politik*, pp. 681-706.)

15. "Royal Highness." In: *Essays on Thomas Mann*, translated by Stanley Mitchell, Merlin Press, London, 1964, pp. 135-7.

16. *"Gespräche mit Georg Lukács,"* pp. 105-10.

17. Ibid., p. 101.

18. Ibid., p. 94.

19. Ibid., p. 45.

20. An ever-recurring theme of Lukács' writings is the

question of the responsibility of the intellectuals. It pre-
dominates in several of his volumes. E.g. *Az írástudók
felelőssége* (The Intellectuals' Responsibility), *Irodalom
és demokrácia* (Literature and Democracy), *Új magyar
Kultúráért* (For a New Hungarian Culture), *Schicksalswende, Existentialisme ou marxisme, Fortschritt und Réak-
tion in der deutschen Literatur, Die Zerstörung der
Vernunft*, etc. A characteristic quotation from one of his
essays:

"The intelligentsia stands at the crossroads. Ought we—
like the intelligentsia of France in the 18th century, and
of Russia in the 19th—to prepare the way and fight for
a new and progressive world epoch, or ought we, like the
German intelligentsia of the first half of the 20th century,
to be helpless sacrifices, weak-willed assistants to the
assistants of a barbaric reaction? There is no question as
to which attitude is *worthy*, and which is unworthy, of the
essence, the knowledge and the culture of the intelligentsia." "Von der Verantwortung der Intellektuellen." In:
Schicksalswende, Aufbau-Verlag, Berlin, 1956, p. 245.

He lays an enormous emphasis on exploring the moral
aspects of general philosophical and aesthetic problems.
Significantly his massive *Aesthetic*—everywhere full of
moral references—reaches its climax in the chapter on
"Der Befreiungskampf der Kunst" (The Liberating Struggle
of Art). (See *Die Eigenart des Ästhetischen*, Luchterhand,
Neuwied-Berlin, 1963, Vol. 2, pp. 675-872.) Thus for
Lukács a work of art devoid of moral significance, not
surprisingly, cannot pass the test of lasting artistic significance.

21. I have discussed some related aspects of Lukács' work in
"Die Philosophie des 'tertium datur' und des Koexistenz-
dialogs", *Festschrift zum Achizigsten Geburtstag von Georg
Lukács*, Luchterhand, Neuwied-Berlin, 1965, pp. 188-207.
22. *Die Seele und die Formen*. Egon Fleischel & Co., Berlin,
1911, p. 189.

23. Ibid., p. 190.
24. Ibid., p. 54.
25. Ibid., p. 177.
26. In 1963, when I returned to him some three hundred foolscap pages of the manuscript that survived in Arnold Hauser's custody, though glad about the survival of an old document, he found that it would be a waste of time re-reading it.
27. One short quotation should suffice to give an idea of the type of style in question:

   Blessed are the ages for which the starry heavens are the map of the roads which can be travelled and which are to be travelled, and whose roads are illuminated by the light of the stars. Everything is new for them, and yet familiar; adventurous, and yet their own property. The world is wide, and yet it is like their own home, for the fire which burns in the soul is of the same nature as the stars. They are sharply separated—the world and the ego, the light and the fire—and yet they will never be eternal strangers to one another; for fire is the soul of every light, and every fire clothes itself in light.

   Die Theorie des Romans. Ein geschichtsphilosophischer Versuch über die Formen der grossen Epik. P. Cassirer, Berlin, 1920, p. 9.
28. Ibid., p. 75.
29. *"Taktika és etika."* (Tactics and Ethics.) In: Georg Lukács: *Schriften zur Ideologie und Politik,* p. 40.
30. *Geschichte und Klassenbewusstsein,* p. 93.
31. It is to be hoped that one day a re-worked and substantially condensed version of this great *"Rohentwurf"* (rough draft) will appear.
32. *Geschichte und Klassenbewusstsein,* p. 39.
33. Ibid., p. 40.
34. Ibid., p. 23.
35. Ibid., p. 27.
36. "A marxista filozófia feladatai az demokráciában." (The

NOTES

Tasks of Marxist Philosophy in the New Democracy. Text
of a lecture delivered at the Congress of Marxist Philosophers in Milan, on 20 December 1947.) Budapest, 1948,
pp. 11-12.

37. *Geschichte und Klassenbewusstsein*, pp. 36-7.
38. *Die Seele und die Formen*, pp. 17 and 38.
39. Ibid., p. 4.
40. Moses Hess und die Probleme der idealistichen Dialektik." In: *Georg Lukács: Schriften zur Ideologie und
Politik,* p. 268.
41. Ibid., pp. 286-7.
42. See several passages of his essay on Moses Hess.
43. *Új magyar kultúráért.* (For a New Hungarian Culture)
Szikra, Budapest, 1948, p. 134.
44. Op. cit. in Note 36.
45. *"Gespräche mit Georg Lukács,"* pp. 78-9.
46. When Lukács, in 1924, was attacked by Zinoviev—who
later himself fell a victim to Stalinism—in the company
of Antonio Graziadei and Karl Korsch, it was held against
them that they were "professors". (Lukács in fact had his
first University Chair in 1945.) The attack went like this:

"If a few more of these professors come and dish out
their Marxist theories, then the cause will be in a bad
way. We cannot, in our Communist International, allow
theoretical revisionism of this kind to go unpunished."
(See pp. 720-21 of *Georg Lukács: Schriften zur Ideologie
und Politik.*)

The fight against intellectuals in the Comintern was justi-
fied in the name of preserving Maxism against revisionism. In fact it signified the replacement of some fundamental tenets of Marxism by the theses of a narrowly
practicist and rigidly dogmatic version of revisionism.

APPENDIX

TRUTH OF A LEGEND[1]

In the past Lukács was known to English readers only
through his essays in criticism, but none of his major
philosophical works on which his aesthetic principles
were founded was available. Thus people were often
forced to rely on mistaken political conjectures, to fill
in the gaps. This is now slowly being remedied with
the publication of one of Lukács' seminal works[2] to
be followed soon by his *Theory of the Novel*, as well
as by *The Young Hegel* and *The Destruction of
Reason* in the not too distant future.

Two of the three volumes under review show us
Lukács the critic at work. The first[3] contains essays—
written in the Thirties and the Forties—in which
Lukács elaborated some of the basic principles of his
aesthetic theory, such as "artistic subjectivity and

objectivity", the "typical versus the statistical average", "realism versus naturalism", "active reflection versus reified objectivity", "narration versus mere description", the "intellectual physiognomy of characters", "literary heritage", "continuity and discontinuity in art", "evocative power", "particularity and immediacy", and the like. All these categories find their ultimate philosophical reference in *History and Class Consciousness* : in the latter's insistence on "the standpoint of totality"—in opposition to the paralysing and distorting "standpoint of particularism"—as well as on the vital importance of appropriate "mediations" in place of crude (naturalistic) "immediacy".

The same æsthetic categories constitute the pillars of Lukács' essays on Solzhenitsyn, written in 1964 and 1969.[4] A short quotation is enough to illustrate this point :

> In the earlier and also more recent naturalist pictures of society . . . the absence of a unified plot must necessarily result in a static description of the characters and a reduction of their human existence to mere particularity, which to be sure usually aims at the average. In the new type of novel which we have been investigating, the very absence of a unified plot results in a highly dynamic narrative and in an internal drama.

Lukács' strength as a critic is inseparable from the philosophical depth and coherence of his categories which enable him to situate a particular literary work or trend in its comprehensive social-historical setting. And since he is fully aware of the need for "specific mediations", his literary analyses do not remain at an abstract philosophical level but, as a rule, successfully explore the manifold individual features which constitute the unique "physiognomy" of exemplary artistic achievements.

In the essay on Solzhenitsyn's novels Lukács makes the point that Lenin's article on party literature "does not at all refer to imaginative literature". The evidence for this thesis is very shaky indeed: a letter by Krupskaya in which, from a distance of many years, she reports that in her recollection Lenin did not intend to include creative literature in the category of party literature. Lenin's text, however, speaks otherwise. For he refers, unmistakably, to the issue of "the freedom of *literary creation*", emphasizing that

> there is no question that literature is least of all subject to mechanical adjustment and levelling . . . in this field greater scope must undoubtedly be allowed for personal initiative, individual inclination, thought and fantasy, form and content.

107

And Lenin's conclusion is that while *mechanical* control is, of course, not admissible, the principle of "party literature" must indeed apply also to the field of creative literature.

This issue graphically illustrates Lukács' dilemma and the necessary limits of his opposition to Stalinist theories and practices: not simply because he must use Lenin's authority in support of his own principle —which pleads for a privileged position of creative literature—but because his defence of literature against bureaucratic interference must assume the form of an extremely problematical principle. If Krupskaya and Lukács were right on this point, Lenin would be clearly in the wrong. For there is nothing objectionable about stipulating—in the Tsarist Russia of 1905 —that writers who want to join the party should accept their share of the common task, in a form which is appropriate to their medium of activity, i.e., which acknowledges the special relationship between literary form and content, as well as the importance of personal initiative, individual inclination and fantasy. The situation is, however, radically different after 1917, when the party is no longer a persecuted minority but the unchallenged master of the country. Thus the real issue is not the relationship between literature and the party but that between the party and the total institutional framework of post-revolutionary society. And no amount of creative freedom in literature could conceivably remedy the contra-

dictions of the latter. Lukács' noble defence of
Solzhenitsyn against opponents who "read into his
works far-fetched political ideas and credit them with
great political impact"—a defence based on the aesthetic argument that literature is political "only in our
sense of a mediation which is frequently very remote,
since between the artistic level of this portrayal and
its indirect effect actual social connections do exist,
but are distantly mediated"—makes out, again, a
special case for literature, desperately minimizing, in
support of this plea, the fact that the works in question
are bound to have a great political impact in a society
which is far from having realised its own programme
of "de-Stalinization".

Which takes us back to the roots of these developments as depicted in Lukács' legendary work, *History
and Class Consciousness*. Its long awaited English
publication is an important literary event: no mean
achievement for a book written nearly 50 years ago.
And if we remember that on the Continent several
pirate editions were and still are being circulated, we
get some measure of the exceptional character of this
work. *History and Class Consciousness* is unquestion-
ably one of the most discussed theoretical works of the

20th century. It also happens to be one of its truly great books. The problems analysed in it are so wide-ranging that it would be futile to attempt a summary. All I may try to do here is to situate this work, historically and intellectually, pointing to its revealing fate and impact.

Strange though it may sound, *History and Class Consciousness* is more topical today than ever before. At the time of its publication, in 1923, a historical period of great upheavals and expectations was reaching its end. This sealed the immediate fate of Lukács' book, which was written during that period and was meant as a critical self-examination—a revolutionary *prise de conscience*—in the aftermath of the failure of the 1919 Commune in Hungary. Accordingly, Lukács insisted on the vital importance of the methodological principle which stipulates that Marxist criticism "must be constantly applied to itself". And he certainly meant it. To give one example, he stressed that the Communist Party ought to be

> a form of organization that produces and reproduces correct theoretical insights by consciously ensuring that the organization has built into it ways of adapting with increased sensitivity to the effects of a theoretical posture. Thus the ability to act, the faculty of self-criticism, of self-correction and of theoretical development all co-exist in a state of constant interaction.

The use of indicatives in place of imperatives should

not mislead us: it did not even impress Zinoviev and the other top-level bureaucrats of the Comintern who condemned Lukács' book in no uncertain words. What angered them most was Lukács' warning that unless the party can genuinely activate the "total personality" of its members, its discipline

> must degenerate into a reified and abstract system of rights and duties and the party will relapse into a state typical of a party on the bourgeois pattern.

And when they looked at the prospects Lukács painted for them they had to feel even more uneasy. For this is how Lukács' description of that pattern ran:

> The party is divided into an active and a passive group in which the latter is only occasionally brought into play and then only at the behest of the former. The "freedom" possessed by the members of such parties is therefore nothing more than the freedom of more or less peripheral and never fully engaged observers to pass judgment on the fatalistically accepted course of events or the errors of individuals. Such organizations never succeed in encompassing the total personality of their members, they cannot even attempt to do so. Like all the social forms of civilization these organizations are based on the exact mechanized division of labour, on bureaucratization, on the precise delineation and separation of rights and duties.

No wonder that the book had to be condemned.

Its impact was enormous, considering the great complexity of many of its analyses which deal with the problems of dialectics and methodology. Men who came under its influence range from Antonio Gramsci to Walter Benjamin, from Ernst Bloch to the young József Révai, from Karl Korsch and Adorno to Lucien Goldmann, from Marcuse and Horkheimer to Béla Fogarasi, from Arnold Hauser and Karl Mannheim to Henri Lefèbvre and Merleau-Ponty, and to many others. Less well known but intellectually equally important was the influence it indirectly exercised on the development of existentialism (including the young Sartre) via Heidegger's main work—*Being and Time* (1927)—which constantly engaged in a critical discussion of various aspects of Lukács' problematic of "reification" without getting involved in explicit polemics. In sociology—especially in the so-called "sociology of knowledge"—the impact was as great as in philosophy and in political theory, and quite a few people tried to utilize Lukács' categories, in France and elsewhere, also in the field of social psychology and psychiatry. Needless to say, the number of those who tried, and failed, to knock it out of existence was also legion.

Undoubtedly the political fate of this work contributed to the growth of its legend. Also, there were many writings—Merleau-Ponty's book *Les Aventures de la dialectique* was neither the first nor the last of them—which singled out for praise some of its most problematical tenets, tendentiously opposing them to other aspects of the same book and of Lukács' work as a whole. But a truly lasting impact cannot be built on political notoriety alone, nor indeed on the ephemeral sensationalism of distorting interpretations.

History and Class Consciousness is a work of great achievements and shortcomings. Some of the latter—e.g., its leftish political messianism, its confused grasp of the dialectical relationship between "subject and object", "alienation and objectification", "reality and reflection", etc.—are subjected to a searching critical analysis by Lukács himself in his new preface, written in 1967. Others no doubt will continue to be debated in years to come. For the most remarkable thing about this book is the vitality of many of its questions, which have acquired an added intensity through the realization of some of the social and intellectual trends which they pinpointed in their earliest forms of appearance. It was this topicality that kept alive the pirate editions mentioned above; for many of the questions formulated by Lukács in these early essays have stubbornly reappeared in recent years on the political agenda. The extraordinary vehemence with which the Right (much concerned with inventing and propagating a "rigorously aggressive" new ideology, against "vag-aries" of the Left) has recently been attacking Lukács and his influence clearly shows how alive the issues involved are.

NOTES

1. Review article published in *New Statesman* 26 February 1971.
2. *History and Class Consciousness* translated by Rodney Livingstone.
3. *Writer and Critic* translated and edited by Arthur Kahn.
4. *Solzhenitsyn* translated by William Graf.

BIOGRAPHICAL DATA

1885

Born on 13 April 1885, as second son of József Lukács and Adél Wertheimer. His elder brother, János (1884-1944) is killed by the Nazis; Pál, his younger brother, dies at the age of three (1889-1892); his sister, Maria, was born in 1887.

His grandfather, Jákob Löwinger (a small artisan) cannot afford to pay for the education of his children. Thus Lukács' father leaves school at the age of fourteen, in 1869, and has his apprenticeship in a Bank at Szeged, South Hungary. A brilliant financial talent and a phenomenal worker (who learns, on his own, several foreign languages in the evenings during the years of his apprenticeship), he wins himself the post of Chief Correspondent at the Anglo-Hungarian Bank in Budapest at the age of eighteen; at twenty-one he is appointed head of an important department at the Hungarian General Credit Bank, and at the age of twenty-five he becomes a Director at the Anglo-Austrian Bank in Budapest. In 1906 he returns to the Hungarian General Credit Bank as its Managing Director which he remains until he is removed by the Horthy regime because of his son's participation in the Commune of 1919. Shortly before his marriage (on 1st July 1883) he changes his name to Lukács, and on 1st May 1899 he is raised to the nobility as József "Szegedi Lukács". (Some of Lukács' early writings are signed in German "Georg von Lukács".) Lukács' mother, though born in Budapest, is brought up in Vienna and has to learn Hungarian after her marriage. Thus, the family language always remains German, which greatly facilitates for Lukács an early acquaintance with German literature and philosophy.

1902/03

Lukács' first articles appear in *Magyar Szalon*. They are written, on theatre, in Alfred Kerr's impressionistic style.

Between 1902/03 he writes five dramas, on the model of Ibsen and Gerhart Hauptmann, but later he burns them and never returns to creative practising literature. His enthusiasm for modern writers is stimulated by a passionate rejection of Max Nordau's book: *Entartung* which labels Baudelaire, Ibsen, Tolstoy and others as "decadence".

1904

With two friends, László Bánóczi and Sándor Hevesi he founds the "Thalia" theatre group. (Hevesi later becomes Director of the Hungarian National Theatre and also publishes some important writings on dramaturgy.) Under the influence of Bánóczi and his father, Lukács deepens his study of philosophy, systematically exploring the works of Kant, and later of Dilthey and Simmel as well.

1906

Between 1902-1906, to gratify his father's wish, he studies Jurisprudence at Budapest University, and he becomes Doctor of Law in 1906, at Kolozsvár (now Cluj) University.

He publishes his first original essay, on "The Form of the Drama", in the short-lived periodical, *Szerda* (Wednesday). Also, he starts publishing in *Huszadik Század* (Twentieth Century): organ of *"Társadalomtudományi Társaság"* (Society of the Social Sciences). Politically he always supports the general direction of this society against the conservatism of the establishment, but philosophically he is strongly opposed to their Anglo-French orientated positivism.

A vital experience for Lukács this year is the publication of Ady's volume: *Uj Versek* (New Poems).

1906/07

Lukács stays in Berlin where he writes, in Hungarian,

the first draft of his monumental *History of the Development of Modern Drama* : the result of six years of intensive theoretical and practical involvement in theatre and drama. He sends his manuscript, from Berlin, to the "Kisfaludy Társaság" (an important literary society, named after two brothers: minor classics of Hungarian literature).

1908

Lukács is awarded the "Krisztina Lukács Prize" of the Kisfaludy Society for his book on modern drama. (A re-elaborated version of this book appears in 1911, at Budapest, in two volumes.)

He publishes his first essay on Ady, in *Huszadik Század*.

An important literary periodical, *Nyugat* (West) is founded in 1908 (ceases publication in 1941) and Lukács becomes a regular contributor (between 1908 and 1917) while remaining a complete outsider to its general direction. Lukács' romantic but passionately radical anti-capitalism is incompatible with the socio-political line of *Nyugat* which champions an "enlightened" bourgeois order, and his philosophical outlook is equally at odds with the impressionistic dilettantism and liberal-positivist eclecticism of the dominating group. They reject Lukács' article on Ady, they write with total incomprehension and hostility about his famous book *The Soul and the Forms* (written and first published in Hungarian) and they attack his few literary comrades in arms. All this strongly contributes to Lukács' decision to seek intellectual alliance and recognition in Germany.

1909

His friend, Dezsö Czigány—Endre Ady's portrait painter—introduces him to the great Hungarian poet.

He is promoted to Dr Phil. at Budapest University. (The Horthy regime in 1920 nullifies his Doctorat, together with that of Jenö Landler—the much admired leader of the faction to which Lukács belonged in the Hungarian Communist Party.)

He meets Béla Balázs (poet, dramatist and critic: later also a major theoretician of the cinema) who remains one of his most intimate friends for a decade.

Lukács publishes the first of a long line of essays on Thomas Mann.

1909/10

At Berlin University he attends the lectures of Georg Simmel and becomes one of his favourite pupils and a regular participant in the "privatissimo" seminars which meet at the philosopher's home.

He writes in these years the majority of the essays which later compose the volumes: *The Soul and the Forms* (published in Hungarian in 1910 and in German in 1911) and *Aesthetic Culture* (published in Hungarian only, in 1913).

He meets Ernst Bloch who becomes a close friend

and exercises a positive influence on Lukács' youthful philosophical development.

1911

With another close friend—the philosopher and art historian Lajos Fülep—he founds a new periodical: *Szellem* (Spirit). Only two numbers appear, both containing contributions by Lukács. Leo Popper—the greatest friend, according to Lukács himself, of his whole life—dies at the age of twenty-five. (Not only his obituary—published in *Pester Lloyd* on 18 December 1911 and republished in 1971 in *Acta Historiae Artium* with an Introduction by Charles de Tolnay—testifies to Lukács' lifelong attachment to Leo Popper but also the pages dedicated to him in the monumental *Aesthetics* of 1963.) Son of the great cellist David Popper, Leo was Lukács' friend from their early childhood and greatly influenced the elaboration of some of the most fundamental concepts of *The Soul and the Forms*. (The introductory essay of this volume—on "The Essence and Form of the Essay"—is in fact a letter to Leo Popper from Florence, dated October 1910.)

1911/12

After spending a few months in Berlin and in Budapest, he moves again to Florence in order to work out the outline of his *Aesthetics*. The latter is intended to be the first introductory part of his general system of philosophy: an introduction to be followed by a *Philosophy of History* and a work on *Ethics*.

Ernst Bloch, who stayed with him at Budapest in 1910, visits him in Florence in the spring of 1912 and persuades him to move to Heidelberg so as to be able to work in a philosophically more favourable environment.

1912/14

In Heidelberg he meets Max Weber and Emil Lask and becomes a close friend of both. (He also meets Toennies, Gundolf and others and remains on good terms with them until the roads divide at the end of the war.)

Greatly encouraged by Bloch, Lask and Weber, he works on his *Aesthetics*. With shorter or longer interruptions he returns to his ever-growing manuscript several times and—unable to bring it to a satisfactory conclusion—definitively abandons the project in 1918.

He attends the lectures of Windelband and Rickert and, although influenced by them to some extent, he already assumes a critical stance. Stressing the multi-dimensionality of adequate categorial systems, he writes on this subject: "Already at the time of my stay in Heidelberg, I have scandalized the philosophers there by saying that the implicit axiom of Rickert's system is the two-dimensionality of the paper on which he writes." (Letter from Budapest, 9 January 1963.)

Lukács is now increasingly influenced by Hegel's objective idealism. At the same time, he is critical of the conservative elements and of the neglect of the individual in the Hegelian systematization of the Philosophy of History. He plans a work which should have been a critical synthesis of Hegel and Kierkegaard, but does not get far in its realization.

He insists on the primacy of Ethics over Philosophy of History. In this spirit he starts writing a dissertation for the position of a Lecturer at Heidelberg University (a "Habilitationsschrift") but, again, he does not succeed in completing it. The theme of this "Habilitationsschrift" is the investigation—in the light of Dostoevsky's work—of the relationship between Ethics and Philosophy of History. (A record of his thoughts on this problematic survives, in a most unlikely form, in some of Lukács' essays on Béla Balázs.)

1914/15

In Heidelberg he writes his famous *Theory of the Novel*, first published in the *Zeitschrift für Aesthetik und Allgemeine Kunstwissenschaft* in 1916, and in book form in 1920. The great art historian Max Dvořák hails it as the outstanding work of the whole "Geisteswissenschaft" (science of the spirit) movement.

He greets the outbreak of the war with unqualified

pessimism and comments with irony on Marianne Weber's account of stories of individual heroism: "The better the worse!". Similarly, while welcoming the prospect of the destruction of the Habsburg, the Hohenzollern and the Tsarist systems, he asks the question with despair: "But who will save us from Western civilization?"

In philosophy, he is extremely sceptical about Husserl's methodology and makes this clear to Max Scheler when the latter visits him in Heidelberg and declares his enthusiasm for Phenomenology.

Lukács meets his first wife, Yelyena Andreevna Grabenko (a Russian "social revolutionary") to whom *The Theory of the Novel* is dedicated. His parents oppose the marriage plan and the highly respectable Max Weber suggests to Lukács to tell them that she is a relative of his, in order to help overcome their objections. They meet her in Vienna and, reluctantly, give their blessing to the marriage which, however, soon turns out to be a complete failure. She remains in Heidelberg when he returns to Budapest and the marriage is also formally dissolved in 1919.

1915/17
Thanks to his father's influence he is not called up for active military service but only for "segédszolgálat" (supplementary service) and works in a censor's office. At the same time he is able to spend, several times, months abroad, mostly in Heidelberg. In harmony

with his general mood and orientation, he writes sympathetic reviews on W. Solovieff (Vladimir Solovyov—the nihilist turned religious mystic) in two consecutive years of *Archiv für Sozialwissenschaft und Sozialpolitik* (1915 and 1916).

With a group of friends he founds what has become to be known as the "Sunday Circle" and regularly presides over its meetings which take place in the home of Béla Balázs. Its members are: Frigyes Antal (art historian, during the Commune of 1919 Deputy Head of the Directorium for Art), Béla Balázs, Béla Fogarasi (philosopher), Lajos Fülep, Tibor Gergely (painter, Anna Lesznai's second husband), Edith Hajós (Béla Balázs' first wife, translator of Lukács' *Studies in European Realism* into English), Arnold Hauser (sociologist and art historian), György Káldor (journalist), Anna Lesznai (poet and novelist, one of Lukács' closest friends; at the time wife of Oszkár Jászi: historian and editor of *Huszadik Század*), Ernö Lorschy (journalist), Karl Mannheim (sociologist), László Radványi (economist, husband of Anna Seghers), Edith Rényi (psychologist, well known under the name of Edith Gyömröi), Emma Ritoók (at the time a close friend of Ernst Bloch, later a supporter of the Horthyite counterrevolution who denounces her former friends in a book entitled *Adventurers of the Spirit*, published in 1922), Anna Schlamadiner (Balázs' second wife), Ervin Sinkó (novelist), Wilhelm Szilasi (philosopher), Charles de Tolnay (art historian),

Eugene Varga (economist) and John Wilde (art historian).

Strongly encouraged by the syndicalist theoretician Ervin Szabó, Lukács and some of his friends from the "Sunday Circle" organize at the beginning of 1917 a series of public lectures in the framework of what they call "A Szellemtudományok Szabad Iskolája" (Free School of the Sciences of the Spirit). The great Hungarian composers Béla Bartók and Zoltán Kodály also participate in this enterprise. (During the Commune Bartók and Kodály—together with Ernö Dohnányi who later moves to the right— preside over the Directorium for Music.)

Also in 1917 Lukács publishes one chapter of his *Aesthetics*— on "Subject-Object Relations in Aesthetics"—in *Logos* in German and in *Athenaeum* in Hungarian.

1917/18

He greets the October revolution with enthusiasm, although it takes some time before the changing socio-political perspectives really modify his philosophical outlook.

In the winter of 1917 and during the spring of 1918 he works on his essays dedicated to Béla Balázs and publishes them in a volume in Hungarian. As in Ady and in Bartók, he sees in Balázs' work "the triumph of dramatic decisions over opportunistic accommodation, the triumph of living in the spirit of 'either-or' over the philosophy of 'one could have it both ways' ". Much of the polemics is directed against the *Nyugat* circle and explicitly against the accommodating line of the important poet and critic Mihály Babits. (He met Babits through the initiative of Ervin Szabó in 1916 when the latter tried to organize writers to protest against the war. Their personal encounter, however, could not bridge the gulf that separated them both philosophically and in their socio-political attitudes.)

1918

Max Weber stays with Lukács at Budapest for a few weeks; in their conversations, in addition to philosophy and aesthetics, the problems of Marxism and socialism in general occupy a central place. This is the last time their relationship is, on the whole—despite some tensions—a harmonious friendship. Their ways radically divide following the events of 1919.

Lukács intensifies his study of Marx and—under the influence of Ervin Szabó—he studies Rosa Luxemburg, Pannekoek, Henriette Roland-Holst and Sorel as well. (His first acquaintance with some works of Marx goes back to his last years in the grammar school. At that time—in 1902—he even joins a Socialist Student Organization, founded by Ervin Szabó. This early interest in Marx is followed by a long spell of more demanding study, between 1906-11, in connection with his interest in the sociology of

literature and in particular in the sociology of drama:
a study consisting partly of reading Marx in the
original, and partly as mediated through the writings
of Toennies, Simmel, Max Weber and others. His
interest in Marx is again renewed at the time of his
intense study of Hegel—1912-15—and in 1913 he
goes as far as suggesting that a proper understanding
and diffusion of Hegel's ideas can only be expected
through the work of Karl Marx. The war years and
the October revolution give an additional impetus
to this interest, culminating in his conversion to
Marxism—both politically and philosophically—in
1918.)

On the 2nd December 1918 he joins the Communist
Party—founded at Budapest only twelve days earlier.
At the time of his joining the party, membership is
still well below one hundred.

1919
A few weeks after Lukács' entry into the party József
Révai—at the time a strong supporter of the sectarian-
vangardist line of Aladár Komját—attacks him and
wants to have "this bourgeois intellectual" expelled
from the party, unsuccessfully. When he is attacked
for his "conservative views", Lukács shows the incred-
ulous Révai a passage from the *Critique of Political
Economy* in which Marx asserts that Homer is an
"unsurpassable example"; discussions about such a
"conservative" attitude initiate a better relationship,

lasting—with great ups and downs—nearly forty years.

Lukács' father is shattered by the collapse of the Austro-Hungarian Empire, the Károlyi revolution, the killing of his old friend: Prime Minister Count István Tisza, and the political radicalization of his son. However, he never ceases to support Lukács personally by all means at his disposal.

During the arrest of the party's Central Committee, Lukács—as a member of the alternative Central Committee—assumes important functions. Later—in March, when the Hungarian Soviet is declared—he becomes Deputy Minister (Dep. People's Commissar) for Education and after the resignation of the social democrat Zsigmond Kunfi in June, he takes over from Kunfi as head of the Ministry.

He undertakes a radical reorganization of cultural life in Hungary and, among other things, sets up a "Research Institute for the Advancement of Historical Materialism". (His lecture on "The Changing Function of Historical Materialism"—published later in *History and Class Consciousness*—is delivered at the opening ceremony of this Institute.)

During the military campaign against the invading forces Lukács is Political Commissar of the 5th Division.

Lukács' first wife spends the months of the Commune at Budapest (mostly with the members of Komját's group, including Révai), but the marriage

General view of Szeged, home-town of the Lukács family.

Synagogue of Szeged where Lukács' uncle was a Talmudist. The young Lukács kept his photograph on his desk as a demonstration against the "practicism" of bourgeois life and of the future in the world of business hoped for by his father.

The photographs on the following pages, representing Lukács and his family, were taken in 1896, on the occasion of the Hungarian "Millennium".

II.

Georg Lukács.

III.

József Lukács.

IV.

Adél Wertheimer Lukács.

János Lukács.

VI.

Mária Lukács.

Ervin Szabó, Lukács' first teacher of Marxism.

Title page of a lecture by Szabó on Socialism delivered at the "Society of the Social Sciences".

VIII.

Lukács at High School.

THÁLIA TÁRSASÁG

Munkáselőadás 1906 deczember 2-án.

REMÉNY.

SZEMÉLYEK:

Johanna, özvegy halászasszony	Báthory Gizella
Károly	a fiai	Sándor Miklós
Barend		Vámos Hugó
Káza, unokahuga	Forgács Rózsi
Cobus	menedékházbeliek	Törzs Jenő
Péter		Olasz Pál
Simon, ács	Sándor József
Mari, a leánya	Berna Margit
Mátyás, a vőlegénye	Rónay Dezső
Jancsa, hajótulajdonos	Beres Márton
Matilde, a felesége	Berendy Margit
Clementina, a leánya	Verő Margit
Kaps, könyvelő	Bálint Lajos
Lucl	halászasszonyok	Judik Etel
Betty		Király Gizi
Jelle, koldus	Kárpáthy Sándor
Egy rendőr	Sándor József

Az előadás délután 3 órakor kezdődik.

Előadás alatt az ajtók zárva maradnak.

Poster of a "Thália" performance for workers. The play is Hajermans' tragedy "Hope".

Sándor Hevesi who founded the "Thália Company" with Lukács and László Bánóczi, and who later became the Director of the Hungarian National Theatre.

X.

The important literary periodical "Nyugat" (West) of which
Lukács was one of the founders.

The greatest single influence on Lukács' early development;
the plebeian revolutionary poet and essayist Éndre Ady.

XII.

Ady's *New Poems* which made an enormous impact on Lukács.

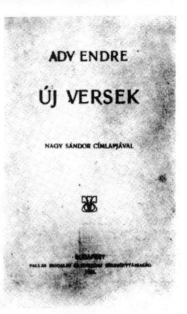

ADY ENDRE

ÚJ VERSEK

NAGY SÁNDOR CÍMLAPJÁVAL

BUDAPEST
PALLAS IRODALMI ÉS NYOMDAI RÉSZVÉNYTÁRSASÁG

Portrait of Ady by Dezsö Czigány, a close friend of Lukács'.

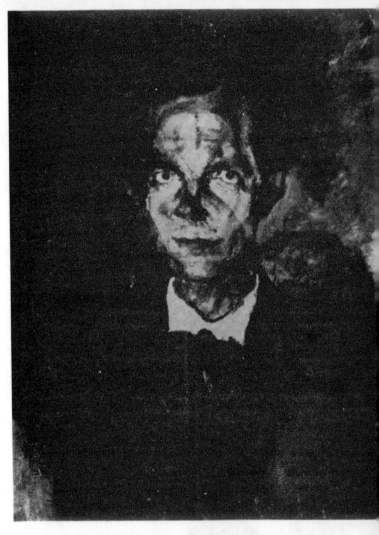

Portrait of Béla Bartók by Róbert Berény (1913).

XIV.

LEÓ POPPER. EIN NACHRUF

von

Gy. Lukács

Die Größe verbietet jede Sentimentalität. Die stumme Sinnlosigkeit seines Dahingehens ist furchtbarer und stärker, als jede Wort von Schmerz oder Klage sein könnte. Was an Möglichkeiten in ihm lag, das ganz zu gestalten, hätte vielleicht die Lebenskraft und die Lebensdauer eines Renaissancemenschen genügt; ihm ward ein kurzes Leben in steter Krankheit zuteil, und die wenigen Stunden der halbwegs konzentrierbaren physischen Kraft mußten für das Schaffen ausreichen. Und dennoch verbietet die lächelnde und ruhige Strenge dieses Lebens jedes Gerede von Hoffnungen, die sich nicht erfüllen konnten, von Wegen, die abgebrochen sind, von Fragmenten. Seine Musik und Malerei konnte sein kranker Körper nicht bis zu Taten bringen, was aber in seinen Essays niedergelegt ist, das ist blühend, mächtig und reich und in sich geschlossen, das verläßt das sinnlos Brüchige seines Lebens, des Lebens: es lebt ein eigenes Leben, es ist zur Form erlöst.

Die Form ist der Gedanke Leó Poppers. Jeder wesentliche Mensch hat nur einen Gedanken; ja es fragt sich, ob der Gedanke überhaupt einen Plural haben kann, ob der wohlfeile Reichtum der Vielheit nicht nur der Oberfläche, dem Ausfall zukommt. Die Form ist das Bindende und das Bannende, das Lösende und das Erlösende seiner Welt. Die Kluft zwischen Leben und Werk, zwischen Welt und Form, zwischen Schaffenden, Gestaltung, Gestalt und Aufnehmen hat noch nie jemand so weit aufgerissen, wie er. Die grauenvolle Inadäquatheit des Lebens, wo alles von blinden Kräften getrieben und von verfälschenden Fiktionen aufgefangen wird, war die Voraussetzung dieser Formenwelt, das notwendige, irreparable Mißverständnis jeder Äußerung, ihre Wiege und ihr Weg: die trennende Einheit von Sein und Form. Aus der Verfälschung jeder Materie durch jedes Ausdrucksmittel entsteht die Form; aus unserer Armut und Beschränkung wird die Erlösung geboren. In Leó Poppers Kunstphilosophie wird die Theorie der Technik zur Metaphysik. Das Urfaktum aller Malerei ist, daß man mit Farben malen muß und daß die Einstoffigkeit der Farben die ganze Vielstoffigkeit der Natur wiedergeben soll, doch nicht kann; diese kühn unternommene Unmöglichkeit und ihr unvermeidliches Scheitern wird in dieser Ästhetik zur kosmischen Vision vom Alltag der Kunst, zum alles umfassenden Formbegriff. So zwingt der Stein den Bildhauer, die auch die Natur sucht und nicht finden kann, zur Einheit des Im-Block-geschlossenen, so wird aus dem Willen zur Buntheit in den Werken der Volkskunst die mystische Vollendung des verborgenen, verlorenen und dennoch überall daseienden Sinnes. Leó Poppers Formbegriff hat alles Beengende und Abstrahierende abgelegt; die Welt der Form ist eine gebende, glückspendende und gebärende, sie ist wahrer, wirklicher und lebendiger als das Leben. (Es ist eine Klassik, wo auch Giotto, Brueghel und Cézanne Klassiker sind.) Die Form ist zur Aktivität erwacht; sie, die Grundlosigkeit selbst, der große Zufall, bricht von der eigenen, unerfahrbaren, metaphysischen Wucht getrieben, ins Leben hinein, schiebt sich zwischen Willen und Werk, verfälscht die Absicht und verwandelt die Tat, auf daß alles klug oder unbewußt falsch Gewollte der Menschen scheitere und aus dieser Niederlage ihres Willens das Wahre entspringe.

Die Form ist die letzte und stärkste Wirklichkeit des Seins. Das an Umfang kleine Werk Leó Poppers schwebt, von der Kraft seiner Formvision getragen, hoch über allen Möglichkeiten seines empirisch gegebenen — Lebens, es ragt in das seinsvolle Leben hinein und findet dort eine Heimat: voll Kraft, Schönheit, Reichtum und Gewandtheit ist alles, was er geschrieben hat, es ist aus der Fülle geboren und mit der edlen Bewußtheit der Fülle gemeistert: aus dem qualvoll Sinnlosen und Fragmentarischen seines Lebens ist kein Schatten auf dieses Leuchten gefallen. Dieser Glanz muß jede Klage dämpfen: die Heldenhaftigkeit, mit der er sein Wesen aus seinem Leben heraushob und zur Wesenheit formte, gebietet Staunen und Stille der Andacht: vor ihr muß jede Trauer tränenlos werden.

Aus Heft. Au. Ung. Tsome 17, 1971

Lukács' obituary of his greatest friend, Leo Popper. (First published in *Pester Lloyd* in 1911.)

Aesthetic Culture.

LUKÁCS GYÖRGY
ESZTÉTIKAI KULTURA
— TANULMÁNYOK —

BUDAPEST
ATHENAEUM IROD. ES NYOMD. RESZVENYT. KIADASA

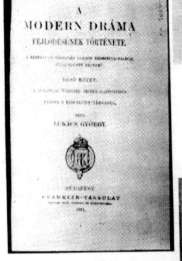

A
MODERN DRÁMA
FEJLŐDÉSÉNEK TÖRTÉNETE

ELSŐ KÖTET.

IRTA
LUKÁCS GYÖRGY

BUDAPEST
FRANKLIN-TÁRSULAT
1911.

History of the
Development of
Modern Drama.

GEORG VON LUKÁCS
DIE SEELE UND DIE
FORMEN / ESSAYS

EGON FLEISCHEL & CO. BERLIN
1911

The Soul and the
Forms.

XVI.

Lukács at the time of moving to Heidelberg.

XVII.

Georg Simmel.

Ernst Bloch.

XVIII.

Max Weber.

View of Heidelberg.

in kennen wäre, wie es es keine Grösse gewesen wur mituteilen, in t
die Entscheidung fällt, geführt haben, wie es die Handlung (E) 25)
direkt vor dem jüngsten Gericht gestohlen wäre te, wo die Tat abge-
wört hat und es nur diejenigen Folgen der Tat geben kann, die in
ihrer rein ethischen Intention ontologisch mitgestzt waren. In der
so
gefassten Entscheidung, in der wahrhaft absoluten etaischen Setzung
kann erst das ethische Subjekt, der Charakter entstehen; aber sein
Entstehen begründet sich eben darauf, dass der Charakter keiner
"Continuität" irgendwelcher "Wirklichkeit" allmählich und die Continuität bewahrend entsteigt, sondern diese radikal annihilierend, zu
ihr völlig heterogen d.h. absolut gesetzt wird. Und diese
absolute Setzung bedingt, mit derselben systematischen Notwendigkeit,
mit der Kants Ding an sich oder Hegels reines Sein gesetzt werden
mussten, dass der absolute Charakter einem ethischen Chaos, dem
Chaos sub specie Ethik, der πρώτη ὕλη der Ethik entgegen-gesetzt
werden muss, dass der Entscheidung dieser Schauer des Abgrundes not-
wendig vorauszugehen hat. /Dass durch diese schroffe Betonung der
Absolutheit jeder einzelnen ethischen Tat und ihres unmittelbaren
Zurückgehens auf das "vor"-ethische Chaos werden die Einheit des
Charakters noch der Zusammenhang der ethischen Sphäre als ganzes
genommen zerrissen wird, kann hier leider nicht ausgeführt werden/

Der andere Typus der Setzung scheint auf dem ersten
Blick eine konkretere Annäherung zum Urgrund zu bedeuten, wie die
soeben charakterisierte reine und autonome Setzungsart. Ist doch das
auffallendste Kennzeichen ihrer Entscheidung, dass, während wir es
in den autonomen Setzungen mit normativen Subjekten zu tun haben,
mit Subjekten die mit dem "Menschen" nicht wesentlich zusammenfal-
len, ja oft nicht einmal zusammen hängen brauchen, es sich hier
um ein dem "Menschen" irgendwie angehörendes, von ihm nicht loslös-
bares Subjekt handelt. "Wir sind" sagt Dilthey "zuerst geschicht-
liche Wesen, ehe wir Betrachter der Geschichte werden," und nur weil
wir jene sind, werden wir zu diesem; Es kann hier jedoch nicht auf
die Konstruierung des Erfassens der Kultur zu der reinen Theorie,
auf die von Verstehen und Erkennen ankommen. Die Berufung auf die
Stellungsnahme zur Kultur muss ein bloss illustrierendes Beispiel
bilden für diese andere Art der Setzung bleiben bei der ein

1/
zit. von A. Stein. Begriff des Geistes bei Dilthey. 45.

Two consecutive pages of Lukács' early *Aesthetics*.

XX.

auf anderem Niveau der "Wirklichkeit" bedeuten wird; die sogenann-
te "natürliche Wirklichkeit", jeden weiteren Prozess, den uns der
Übergang zur Kultur zu einem Typus der Kultur entstehen lag, vor
allem die Frage, in wiefern dieses Angreifen der Kultur auch zur
Wissenschaft werden kann, gehört nicht hieher; die Andeutung ihres
Subjektbegriffes und ihrer Gegenstandsstruktur musste nur die Mög-
lichkeit dieser anderen Setzungsart kurz beleuchten. Auch die"natürliche Wirklichkeit" wurde sehr selten auf ihre Struktur und syste-
matische Funktion hin untersucht. Entweder wurde sie mit dem unaus-
sagbaren "Ver" der Setzung gleichgestellt, oder ihre Urgliederung
der Psychologie überwiesen. Dass die erste Annahme falsch ist, er-
weist sich schon daraus, dass es sich bei dem Chaos um eine gestalt-
lose Setzungsnotwendigkeit handelt, während die"natürliche Wirklichkeit", die Welt der "natürlichen Einstellung", die Erlebniswirklichkeit, wie wir sie in Zukunft nennen werden, eine bestimmte Art des
Lebens oder konkret-gegebenen Welt, das hic et nunc ist, über dessen
konkrete Gegebenheit und Aussagbarkeit kein Zweifel bestehen kann,
wenn seine spezifische Gegenständlichkeit auch noch nicht ergründet
ist. Es ist aber ebenso falsch, diese Ergründung der Psychologie
überlassen zu wollen. Denn die Gegenstandssphäre der Psychologie
- einerlei wie sonst über ihre Methode und Stellung zum System ge-
dacht wird - der Struktur oder Gesetzeszusammenhang, der die soge-
nannten seelischen Erscheinungen, als solche, mit einander ver-
knüpft. Die Psychologie ist deshalb geradeso eine Homogenisierung,
eine Abstraktion, eine Projektion auf eine bestimmte Ebene der Er-
kennbarkeit, wie irgendeine andere Art der Wissenschaft und ist nicht
einmal dem Stoffe ihrer Untersuchung nach an den der Erlebniswirklichkeit gebunden. Der Schein eines intimeren Zusammenhanges zwischen Erlebniswirklichkeit und Psychologie entsteht aus der Unge-
klärtheit der Funktion des Erlebnisses in Beiden. Für die Psychologie ist das Erlebnis der Stoff der Untersuchung; die Erlebnisse
werden von der Valenz ihrer gegenständlichen Bezogenheiten frei
d.h. diese kommen nur insofern in Betracht als sie für die Struktur
der Erlebnisse, für ihre Einordenbarkeit in psychologische Zusammen-
hänge von Belang sind und sie werden nun auf diesem so erreichten
Niveau ihrer Vergleichbarkeit miteinander, ihrer Einordenbarkeit in
übergreifende Psychologien, ihrer Subsumierbarkeit unter Gesetze

The corrections are in Lukács' handwriting.

LUKÁCS GYÖRGY
BUDAPEST, V.
BELGRÁD RAKPART 2. V. EM. 5
Telefon: 186-366

Budapest, 1969.12.2.

Kedves Mészáros !

Köszönöm kedves levelét. ~~Sajnos~~ Közben
a tanulmánykötetet is megkaptam. Sajnos
még nem tudtam elolvasni, még a Maga
cikkét sem, mert az utolsó hetekben
nemcsak az Ontológia uj elvi bevezető
fejezete foglalt el, hanem a rendesnél
nagyobb tömegü külföldi látogatók is.
Remélhetőleg hamarosan kikerülök eb-
ből a hullámvölgyből és elolvasha-
tom a cikket, amely nagyon érdekel.
A kivánt könyveket a Jogvédő Irodán
keresztül elküldöm Magának. Kérem fel-
használás után küldje vissza őket,
mert nincs belőle több példányom.

Az Ontológia uj bevezetőjén most dol-
gozom. Remélem az év végére elkészü-
lök vele. Akkor hozzálátok a többi
szöveg átirásához, amivel remélhetőleg nyárra készen leszek.

Ami a régi Esztétikát illeti, nagyon
nehéz a régi tervet pontosan rekonstruál-
ni. Az első rész lett volna: "Die ästhetische Setzung". A második rész beveze-
tőjéül a Logos-cikk volt tervezve, azt
követte volna a "Geschichtlichkeit und
Zeitlosigkeit des Kunstwerks". Ezután
a második részben még két fejezet kö-
vetkezett volna: "Individualität und
Überpersönlichkeit des Kunstwerks" és
"Das erreichte Werk als Formenkomplex".

./.

"As to the old *Aesthetics*, it would be very difficult to
reconstruct the original plan exactly. *Die ästhetische Setzung*
should have constituted Part One. The essay published in
Logos (Die Subjekt-Objekt Beziehung in der Ästhetik, 1917)
was planned as the introduction to Part Two, and it should
have been followed by *Geschichtlichkeit und Zeitlosigkeit des
Kunstwerks*. Part Two should have contained the chapters on
Individualität und Uberpersönlichkeit des Kunstwerks and on
Das erreichte Werk als Formenkomplex.

XXII.

A harmadik rész a recepetivitás különböző tipusaival foglalkozott volna. Mindez persze csak emlékezés, mely nem is lehet pontos, mert irás közben a terv nem egyszer változott. A megiráshoz Heidelbergben fogtam hozzá 1912-ben. A háboru kitörése, a "Theorie des Romans" megirása, budapesti katonai szolgálatom félbeszakitotta a munkát, de 1916 után egészen 1918-ig még mindig nem adtam fel a megirást.

Eörsi Pista most jött meg, a napokban fogok vele beszélgetni és remélem, még néhány részletet fogok hallani Magáról és terveiről.

Meleg üdvözlettel

Lukács György

"Part Three was to analyse the various types of receptivity. All this is, of course, only a recollection which cannot be exact since in the course of writing the plan had changed more than once. I started writing it at Heidelberg in 1912. The work was interrupted by the outbreak of the war, by my writing *Die Theorie des Romans* and by my military service at Budapest, but I had taken up the plan again after 1916 and had not abandoned it definitively until 1918".

Lukács in 1914.

Lukács and his mother in 1915.

Lukács towards the end of 1916.

Motto of Lukács' book on Balázs.

Was klagst du über Feinde?
Sollten solche je wenden Freunde,
Denen das Wesen, wie du bist,
Im Stillen ein ewiger Vorwurf ist.

Westöstlicher Diwan.

Arnold Hauser (left) and Karl Mannheim in August 1916.

XXVI.

LUKÁCS GYÖRGY

BALÁZS BÉLA

ÉS AKIKNEK NEM KELL

ÖSSZEGYŰJTÖTT
TANULMÁNYOK

1 9 1 8
KNER IZIDOR KIADÁSA GYOMA

Lukács' book in
defence of Balázs.

Béla Balázs.

Portrait of Lajos Fülep by Lajos Tihanyi (1917).

Arnold Hauser.

XXVIII.

Vilhelm Szilasi and Tibor Déry.

Gyula Illyés.

XXIX.

Lukács as People's Commissar for Culture (1919).

XXX.

Proletárdiktatura és kultura.

Proletártestvérek!

A proletáriátus osztálykülzelmének régóthasznú szal is próbálták hkicsinyelni az őket megsemmisítéssel fenyegető mozgalmat, hogy kizárólag gyomorkérdéseknek minősítették azokat a célokat, amelyekért a proletáriátus harcba indult. Igy próbálták meg az ellentét segítségével kiemelni a maguk "kulturáit", magasabbrendü" voltát. Már elmult — a proletáriátus ezerjének és egységének mondanak köszönetet, hogy elmult — az az idő, amikor a kérdés felől vitatkozni még érdemes volt. Ma nem kell többé érveket csoportositania a proletáriátusnak, hogy a kulturára való érettségét bizonyitsa. Kezébe vette sorsának intézését és tetteikkel bizonyitja, hogy milyen kulturát képes teremteni.

Mert a proletáriátus eme kulturát teremtő tette az egyedüli kiut, amely ma a világ számára nyitva áll. Ahogy a termelésben egy a véglettekig lerongyolódott, már a tönk szélén álló gépezetet vett át a proletáriátus, ugy van ez a kulturában is. Szó sincs arról, hogy valami kimondhatatlan eleven értékek kincseháza volna a kezükben. Szó sincs arról, hogy egy nagy, fölfelé vezető fejlődésbe kapcsolódtunk bele és fölnünk kellene, hogy a mi vezetősünk alatt lehanyatlik. Ellenkezőleg. Ahogy lerongyolódott termelést vettünk át a kapitalizmustól, ugy egy lerongyolt kulturát is.

Proletártestvérek!

A kapitalizmus kulturáját halálra itélte maga a tőkés termelési rend. Mert az nemcsak a munkásokat tette szabaddá abban a marxi kettős értelemben, hogy szaba-

dók, mert személyük fölött szabadon rendelkeznek és egyaxxxmind "szabadok" mindentől, amit, munkaerejüket kivéve, a piacra vihetnének, hanem elvágta a kulturát igazi forrásától is: a közönségtől élők szabad együttmüködésétől. A kapitalizmus nemcsak a munkásságot hajtotta a kizsákmányolás igájába, hanem magukat a kizsákmányolókat is, tőlük is ... fajtái ... kedő osztályok számára, hogy ... élhessenek magasrendü, a kulturának szentelt életet, addig a kapitalizmus ott csak elszigetelt egyének és nem kizsákmányolt osztályok számára tette lehetővé. Az igazi kultura ezért mindig hontalan volt a kapitalizmus világában. Az uralmat az üres semmittevők bágyadt idegeinek csiklandozására vagy az agyonhajszolt kapitalista főnökök kimerült idegeinek lecsillapitására szolgáló parazita-termékek ragadják magukhoz. Ami kevés jó van, az nem kell senkinek. A kapitalizmusra magára áll az, amit hivei a proletárság küzdelmének vetnek szemére: hogy gyomorkérdés lesz minden kérdésből. A kapitalizmus az első és reménhetőleg az utolsó kultura az emberiség történetében, amelynek központjában a megélhetés, egyedül a megélhetés állott.

A proletáriátus győzelmének kulturális fontossága éppen abban áll, hogy ezt a kérdést megfosztja központi helyzetétől. A megélhetés, az emberhez méltó élet elvesziti bitorolt fontosságát. Magától értetődő lesz mindenki számára és ezáltal lehetővé lesz, hogy mindenki életének középpontjá-

Karl Mannheim shortly after leaving Hungary; Lukács had appointed him to a Chair at Budapest University during the Commune.

Thomas Mann and his wife (on left) as guests of Lukács' father in Budapest (April 1922).

XXXII.

GEORG LUKÁCS

GESCHICHTE

UND

KLASSENBEWUSSTSEIN

STUDIEN ÜBER MARXISTISCHE DIALEKTIK

DER MALIK-VERLAG / BERLIN

itle page of the first edition of *History and Class Consciousness.*

Ladislaus Rudas:

Die Klassenbewußtseinstheorie von Lukács.

(Fortsetzung und Schluß)*)

4. Eine Wahlverwandtschaft.

In zwei Hinsichten kann man, wie wir gesehen haben, dem Gen. L. eine große Konsequenz nicht abstreiten: erstens in Hinsicht der Inkonsequenz, mit der aus materialistischen Voraussetzungen Marx' idealistische Schlüsse zieht; zweitens, was bei einem Schriftsteller, dessen Haupteigenschaft die Inkonsequenz ist, nicht zu erwarten wäre, in Hinsicht der Beharrlichkeit, mit der er seinen idealistischen Voraussetzungen treu bleibt, aus denen er nie materialistische, sondern immer unve ʼlschte idealistische, agnostizistische, mystische Schlüsse zieht.

Er, der an einigen Stellen seines Buches von der notwendigen Begriffsmythologie der bürgerlichen Soziologen spricht, mißachtet diese seine eigene Warnung und ist selbst nichts anderes als ein Begriffsmythologe, wie wir das oben bei seinem Begriff des Klassenbewußtseins konstatierten und auf Schritt und Tritt seines Buches konstatieren können. Diese Begriffsmythologie ist aber unvermeidlich bei idealistischen Voraussetzungen, ist doch der ganze Idealismus im Grunde genommen nichts anderes als eine Mythologie, nicht umsonst ist er wahlverwandt mit der Religion.

Die allgemeine idealistische Voraussetzung des Gen. L. ist die, daß er einen Gegensatz konstruiert zwischen Natur und Geschichte, einen Gegensatz, der nicht da ist und nicht da sein kann. Das haben wir konstatiert bei seiner Annahme, daß die Dialektik nur in der Gesellschaft, nicht aber in der Natur Geltung habe. Und alle seine weiteren Folgerungen fließen aus dieser seiner Grundvoraussetzung. Der von ihm konstruierte Gegensatz zwischen Natur und Gesellschaft treibt ihn weiter: er ist genötigt, einen weiteren Gegensatz zu konstruieren zwischen dem gewöhnlichen Menschen, so wie er leibt und lebt und im alltäglichen Leben sich benimmt, und dem „geschichtlichen", „geschichtlich bedeutsam handelnden" Menschen. Dann zwischen dem alltäglichen, gewöhnlichen Bewußtsein und dem „(zugerechneten) Klassenbewußtsein" usw.

Daß die idealistische Grundauffassung eines Denkers nicht auf die Grundlagen seiner Theorie beschränkt bleiben kann, das

---

*) Siehe S. 669 Arb.-Literatur Nr. 10.

65

A page of Rudas' attack on *History and Class Consciousness*, 1924.
XXXIV.

The young Révai.

The young Korsch.

The poet Attila József during the revolution of 1918, and at the time of his encounter with Lukács at Vienna in 1925.

XXXVI.

Lukács was a
major contributor
to both
periodicals.

INTERNATIONALE
LITERATUR
DEUTSCHE BLÄTTER

7

9. JAHRGANG 1939

DAS WORT

LITERARISCHE MONATSSCHRIFT
REDAKTION: BERTOLT BRECHT, LION FEUCHTWANGER, WILLI BREDEL

2

JOURGAZ-VERLAG MOSKAU/3.JAHR 1938

UJ HANG

IRODALMI ÉS TÁRSADALMI FOLYÓIRAT

Felelős szerkesztő:
BARTA SÁNDOR

Főmunkatársak:

Balázs Béla, Bölöni György, Fábry Zoltán, Forbáth Imre,
Gábor Andor, Gergely Sándor, Lukács György, Madzsar
József, Vass László

MEGJELENIK HAVONTA EGYSZER

1938 Január   Első évfolyam   Első szám

First issue of *Új Hang* (New Voice).

XXXVIII.

LUKÁCS GYÖRGY

IRÁSTUDÓK
FELELŐSSÉGE

IDEGENNYELVŰ IRODALMI KIADÓ
MOSZKVA 1944

The Responsibility of Intellectuals; Lukács first book in
Hungarian after an interval of twenty years.

View from Lukács' study, looking south-west.

The Faculty of Philosophy at Budapest University.

XL.

Waterfront on the Danube, with Mount St Gellért in the
background, opposite Lukács' home.

On this page and on the next, Lukács in 1948.

XLII.

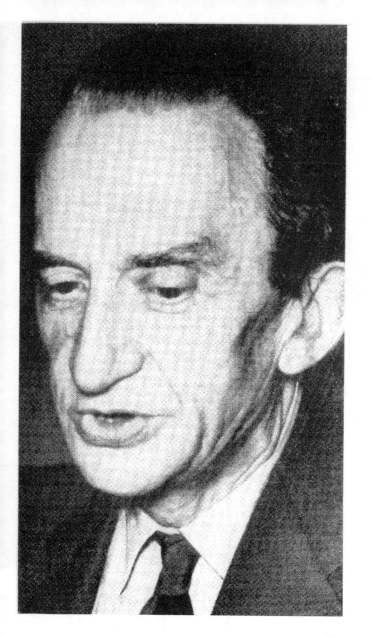

XLIII.

József Révai at the time of the "Lukács Debate".

Literature and Democracy, one of Lukács' books at the centre of the attacks.

Lukács in 1949.

LUKÁCS GYÖRGY

Új magyar kultúráért

SZIKRA

For a New Hungarian Culture—the other main target.

Lukács in 1955.

XLVI.

Lukács in 1956.

The hills of the Mátra and the rest-house of the Hungarian Academy of Science where Lukács, a passionate walker, used to spend his holidays.

Lukács and his wife in 1956.

A note in Lukács' handwriting.

Lukács in 1956.

L.

Lukács' wife, Gertrud Bortstieber in 1956.

Lukács in 1960.

Lukács and his sister in 1962.

Lukács in 1965.

LIV.

Lukács in 1969.

Lukács in 1970.

LVI.

Lukács in 1970 (Photo by E. Vattay).

An interview with Áron Tóbiás in 1970 (Photo K. Koffán).

LVIII.

LIX.

Portrait of Lukács by Georg Eisler (1970).

Lukács receives the Joliot-Curie Memorial Medal from
Romesh Chandra.

Lukács receives
the Goethe Prize
at Budapest from
the Mayor of
Frankfurt.

Lukács' last public appearance at the Bartók festivities.

Béla Bartók.

On this page and the next, Lukács' last photographs.

LXIV.

is irremediably broken down by then. After the collapse she has to hide from Horthy's men until she is able to flee the country, with the help of Lukács' father.

Many of Lukács' old friends—including Frigyes Antal, Béla Balázs, Béla Fogarasi, Arnold Hauser (after a short spell in jail), Anna Lesznai, Karl Mannheim, Ervin Sinkó, Eugene Varga, John Wilde —leave the country, others (like Wilhelm Szilasi and Charles de Tolnay) follow them later.

Lukács carries on illegal work after the overthrow of the Commune in August and September, in association with Ottó Korvin, executed in 1920 (whom he later cites as an example of the heroic-ascetic type of revolutionary), hiding in the house of the photographer Olga Máté. (Charles de Tolnay acts at times as courier for him.)

At the end of September, through the mediation of an old friend—the sculptor Márk Vedres—an English officer, in exchange for a very substantial sum of money provided by Lukács' father (who has to borrow a good deal of it), takes him out of the country, disguised as his personal chauffeur. (Lukács was never able to drive a car.)

In October he is arrested in Vienna and the Horthy Government asks for his extradition. (He is condemned to death in absentia.)

A group of intellectuals intervenes in his favour with the Austrian Government and publishes an

appeal in *Berliner Tageblatt* on the 12th November.
The signatories are: Franz Ferdinand Baumgarten,
Richard Beer-Hoffmann, Richard Dehmel, Paul
Ernst, Bruno Frank, Maximilian Harden, Alfred
Kerr, Heinrich Mann, Thomas Mann, Emil
Praetorius and Karl Scheffler.

The extradition demand is rejected and Lukács is
released towards the end of December.

1920

He marries the great love of his early youth, Gertrud
Bortstieber. (Three years his elder, she is a frequent
visitor to the Lukács family around 1902, being a
close friend of Rózsi Hofstädter, the wife of Zsigmond
Kotányi: the most intimate friend of Lukács' father.
The young Lukács falls deeply in love with her but
at the time she takes no notice of him and marries the
mathematician Imre Jánossy who later dies of tuber-
culosis.) They fall in love in 1918/19 and marry in
1920, after she joins him in Vienna. They have a
daughter, Anna, and they have to bring up—often
under conditions of great hardship—three children. (Imre Jánossy's two sons: Lajos, the world
famous physicist, and Ferenc, an engineer turned (a
very original) economist, are infants when their
father dies). An economist by training, with a profound sensitivity for music and literature, Gertrud
unites in her person the qualities of great practical
wisdom and sense of realism with an irrepressibly

serene outlook on life and a radiating warmth of character. They have a wonderful marriage, and Lukács' great works—including *History and Class Consciousness*: appropriately dedicated to Gertrud Bortstieber—are unthinkable without her.

Lukács is very actively involved in party work, becoming deputy leader of the Landler faction.

His political line is strongly leftist and he is criticized by Lenin for his article on parliamentarism ("Zur Frage des Parlamentarismus", published in *Kommunismus* in 1920).

Horthy agents abduct several Hungarian emigrés from Vienna and Lukács is warned to take precautions. He buys himself a pistol which he keeps until 1933 when (after a Nazi search at his home, luckily in his absence) he throws it into the river Spree. Contrary to accusations according to which "Lukács terrorized the intellectuals during the Commune, pointing his gun at them while questioning them", this is the only weapon he has handled in his lifetime.

In December 1920 he presents a report on "World Reaction and World Revolution" at the second South-East Conference of the Communist Youth International at Vienna (published in 1921).

1920/21
Co-Editor of the important theoretical journal: *Kommunismus*, an organ of the Comintern. Several

of the essays later collected in *History and Class Consciousness* are written in this period and first published in *Kommunismus*.

Representing the Landler faction, he takes part in the discussions of the Third Congress of the Comintern in Moscow and meets Lenin personally. He always describes this encounter as one of the great formative experiences of his life.

Politically his line shows a certain duality: a leftist "Messianic" and rather sectarian approach to the problems of world revolution (he is a supporter, indeed theoretician, of the "March Action" in 1921) and at the same time a highly realistic, non-sectarian assessment of the prospects of socialist development in Hungary. (In the latter respect Landler's influence is crucial.)

He embarks on a systematic study and rethinking of the works of Marx and Lenin the results of which become evident in *History and Class Consciousness* and in his book on *Lenin*.

1922

Thomas Mann visits Lukács' family at Budapest in the spring of 1922. After this visit he goes to Vienna where he meets Lukács for the first time. (Thomas Mann's impressions of their long conversation are well known from Mann's account of it.)

Lukács publishes an article entitled "Yet Again the Politics of Illusions" (Noch einmal Illusionspolitik) in which he condemns, in the strongest possible terms, the advance of bureaucratization and authoritarianism in the party. The article is, significantly, published in Ladislaus Rudas' book: *Adventurism and Liquidationism: Béla Kún's Politics and the Crisis of the Hungarian Communist Party*. Rudas is at the time a supporter of the Landler faction. Just before Christmas Lukács puts the finishing touches to one of the greatest philosophical works of the twentieth century: his essay on "Reification and the Consciousness of the Proletariat", the centrepiece of *History and Class Consciousness*.

1923

Lukács publishes, at Malik Verlag: Berlin, *History and Class Consciousness* which remains by far his most influential book to date.

Ernst Bloch publishes a warm appraisal in an essay entitled: *Aktualität und Utopie: zu Lukács "Geschichte und Klassenbewusstsein"*.

At the end of 1923 Karl Korsch—a friend of Lukács at the time—publishes his *Marxism and Philosophy* which shows a similarity of approach to Lukács' essays published first in *Kommunismus* and in *Die Internationale* (edited by Korsch) as regards some fundamental philosophical and political issues. (Several—but by no means all—of these essays from *Kommunismus* and *Die Internationale* are incorporated in some form into *History and Class Conscious-*

ness.) On the basis of this affinity the following year they are branded and condemned together as "revisionists".

The factional struggle within the Hungarian party sharpens.

1924

Lenin dies in January and the bid for a Stalinist control of both the Soviet party and of the Comintern is intensified.

History and Class Consciousness is attacked from two—opposed—directions: Karl Kautsky attacks it in an article published in *Die Gesellschaft* (June 1924) and the Russian party philosopher A. Deborin condemns it in *Arbeiterliteratur*, in an essay entitled "Lukács und seine Kritik des Marxismus".

Expressing the drastically changing relation of forces within the party and within the Comintern, Ladislaus Rudas—who used to be a supporter of Lukács'—radically alters his position and violently attacks *History and Class Consciousness* in a book-length essay published, in several instalments, in *Arbeiterliteratur* (Nos. 9, 10 and 12, 1924). The programmatic motto of Rudas' attack is, significantly, a quote from Lenin's *Materialism and Empirio-Criticism* which reads: "Beweise und Syllogismen allein genügen nicht zur Widerlegung des Idealismus. Nicht um theoretische Argumente handelt es sich hier." (Proofs and deductions are not enough for eradicating idealism. We are not concerned here with theoretical arguments.)

The climax is reached at the 5th World Congress of the Communist International, in June and July 1924, when Lukács is attacked by Bukharin and Zinoviev.

Lukács publishes his book on Lenin.

1925/26
In 1925 he publishes a severe critique of the mechanistic technological determinism of Bukharin's book on historical materialism in the *Archiv für die Geschichte des Sozialismus und der Arbeiterbewegung* ("Grünberg Archiv" for short).

His attention is directed towards the elaboration of the problems of Marxist dialectic in relation to the economic foundations of capitalist society, anticipating in two major essays—on Lassalle (1925) and on Moses Hess (1926)—the problematic of *The Young Hegel* (1935/38).

József Révai publishes an enthusiastic review of *History and Class Consciousness* in the *Grünberg Archiv*, but he does not go into the question of politico-philosophical controversy surrounding the book.

Lukács meets the young Attila József in Vienna and he is the first to recognize the significance of the work of this great poet for world literature. (As József himself writes to his sister from Vienna: "Anna

Lesznai, Béla Balázs and György Lukács think of me
as a great poet; in particular the latter, who says
that I am the first proletarian poet who possesses the
qualities of world literary import".)

Karl Korsch is expelled from the party in 1926
and, thus, Lukács becomes even more isolated with
his views within the international communist movement.

1927
His father dies at Budapest, at the age of 74. (His
mother had died ten years earlier.)

1928
Jenö Landler dies of heart attack and it falls upon
Lukács to prepare the theses representing the socio-
political perspectives of the party. They become
famous as "The Blum Theses" and they anticipate
the strategy of the "Popular Front".

Lukács' literary activity is confined to writing a
few review articles, mainly in the *Grünberg Archiv*.

1929
Lukács spends three months (directing underground
party work) in Hungary.

His "Blum Theses" are defeated, thanks to the
support enjoyed by the Kún faction within the
Comintern. (The "Open Letter of the Executive of
the Communist International" addressed to the

Hungarian party commands that "the fire must be concentrated on the anti-Leninist theses of comrade Blum who replaced the Leninist theory of proletarian revolution by a half-socialdemocratic liquidationist theory.") Lukács is forced to publish a self-critical declaration in *Uj Március* and his defeat marks the end of his direct involvement in politics for nearly three decades.

The Austrian Government serves an expulsion order on Lukács. Thomas Mann intercedes in his favour in a moving letter. The expulsion order is revoked, but Lukács leaves Vienna—where he lived between 1919-1929—for good.

1929/31

In Moscow he works at the Marx-Engels-Lenin Institute, directed by D. Riazanov. The latter shows him the full typescript of Marx's *Economic and Philosophical Manuscripts of 1844* before publication: it has a major impact on Lukács' intellectual development. In the same period he gets acquainted with Lenin's *Philosophical Notebooks*, published in 1929/30 under the title of *Lenin Miscellanies IX. & XII*. These writings, too, greatly contribute to the modification of his conception of Hegel and of his view of "subject-object relations", of epistemology and of the relationship between the work of art and social reality.

This is the only period in Lukács' life—since 1905

—which he is able to dedicate entirely to research and study, undisturbed both by the pressure of writing for publication and the demands of political activity. Thus, he can lay the foundations of much of his later work.

1931/33

He moves to Germany, living in Berlin until the Nazis come to power.

Vice-President of the Berlin group of the German Writers' Association and a leading member of the League of Proletarian-Revolutionary Writers.

In 1931/32 he works out the "Outlines of a Programme of the League of Proletarian-Revolutionary Writers".

He takes a very active part in the discussions concerning the methods of socialist literary representation, in the spirit of his conception of "great realism".

In 1933 he publishes "Mein Weg zu Marx" (My Road to Marx) in *Internationale Literatur*.

When he learns that the Nazis are looking for him, he escapes from Germany and returns to Moscow.

1933/35

On his return to Moscow Béla Kún and his supporters try to prevent the settling of Lukács and his family. He starts a sit-down strike on the steps of the Comintern building (frequented by many foreigners who know Lukács well): his defiance quickly obtains the desired end.

He becomes scientific collaborator in the Institute of Philosophy of the Soviet Academy of Sciences.

He is working on *The Young Hegel* (completed only in the winter of 1937/38): a project conceived during the period of rethinking his earlier philosophical views in the light of the *Paris Manuscripts* and the *Philosophical Notebooks*. (Also in Berlin, between 1931/33, he tried to work on this project but could not get very far with it.)

In the field of literary criticism he is working in close collaboration with Mikhail Lifshitz. (They became friends in 1929, at the Marx-Engels-Lenin Institute, and Lukács later dedicates *The Young Hegel*—both in the Vienna/Zürich edition of 1948 and in the East German edition of 1954—to Lifshitz, in defiance of the accusations of "cosmopolitanism" levelled against his old friend.) Their organ is *Literaturny Critique* (suppressed in 1940) and their main target is the "Proletcult" line whose principal spokesmen are Fedyeev and Yermilov. Lukács is intellectual leader of the *Literaturny Critique* whose inner circle comprises, in addition to Lifshitz, also I. Satz and Usiyevitch.

Lukács is also involved in a confrontation with the Hungarian group of "Proletcult" writers (Sándor Barta, Antal Hidas: Béla Kún's son-in-law, Béla Illés, Lajos Kiss, Emil Madarász, János Matheika,

Máté Zalka, and others): the same group which condemned Attila József, with devastating results, in an official document as a "petit bourgeois who is trying to find a solution to his inner crisis in the camp of fascism".

In aesthetic theory—again in close collaboration with Liftshitz—Lukács is working on Marx's literary heritage, elaborating the rough general outlines of a systematic Marxist Aesthetic.

In this period he carries on the debate on expressionism—started earlier in Berlin and concluded only towards the end of the 'thirties—in which he crosses swords, among others, with Bertolt Brecht and Ernst Bloch.

1935/38

He completes *The Young Hegel* and submits it as a Doctoral Thesis. He is promoted to "Doctor of the Philosophical Sciences" by the Soviet Academy of Sciences.

Another major work completed by Lukács in this period (1936/37) is *The Historical Novel*.

The newly adopted strategy of the "Popular Front" improves Lukács' situation, facilitating—even if only temporarily—his "partisan struggle" against "Proletcult" and the Zhdanovist version of "socialist realism".

In January 1938 a new Hungarian periodical appears in Moscow: *Uj Hang* (New Voice). Its

Editorial Board is composed of Béla Balázs, Sándor Barta (Chief Editor of the first issue), György Bölöni, Zoltán Fábry, Imre Forbáth, Andor Gábor (one of Lukács' most intimate and faithful friends, Chief Editor from the second issue onwards), Sándor Gergely, György Lukács, József Madzsar and László Vass. Lukács plays a crucial part in determining the general orientation of this periodical. He is also a member of the Editorial Board of *Internationale Literatur* since 1935.

1939/40

In the worsening general political situation the old ideological struggle is reopened in the sharpest possible form. The Fadyeev-Yermilov group obtains the support of the top-level party hierarchy and takes over control of the Writers' Association.

The *Literaturny Critique* is suppressed and Lukács is deprived of the vehicle for the diffusion of his ideas in Russian.

He publishes his essay entitled "Volkstribun oder Bürokrat" (Tribune of the People or Bureaucrat) in *Internationale Literatur*. It is the sharpest and most penetrating critique of bureaucratization published in Russia during the Stalin period (and recognized as such by Leo Kofler (Jules Dévérité) in an article published in 1952 : i.e. before the announcement of the programme of "destalinization").

1941

Lukács is arrested and kept in jail for months. His questioners try to extort from him—without success —a confession to the effect that he has been since the early 'twenties a "Trotskyist agent". He is released only as a result of the personal intervention of Dimitrov (then General Secretary of the Comintern) who receives many representations on Lukács' behalf from German, Austrian, French and Italian intellectuals, as well as from some of his old Hungarian friends, all resident at the time in the Soviet Union.

He publishes essays on Hungarian and German literature. Outstanding among them are his "Faust Studies", published in *Internationale Literatur*.

Uj Hang ceases publication.

1942/44

Lukács' friendship with Révai is renewed after Révai leaves the Comintern where he was working—also as personal secretary to Béla Kún—between 1934/37. Révai's excellent studies on Hungarian literature and history, published mainly in *Uj Hang*, are conceived in the course of long conversations with Lukács. Their friendship is intensified during the war years and remains harmonious until 1949, time of the "Lukács debate".

Lukács gives lectures in German and Hungarian prisoners of war camps.

In the summer of 1944 he publishes *Irástudók felelössége* (The Responsibility of Intellectuals): a volume of essays on Hungarian literature and history, written beween 1939/41 and first published in *Uj Hang*, with an Introduction dated March 1944. This is his first volume to appear in Hungarian after an interval of twenty years. (His last was the little book on *Lenin*, published also in Hungarian in Vienna in 1924.)

1945

He has the possibility of settling permanently either in Germany or in Hungary. He chooses the latter and never regrets his choice, not even under the cross-fire of the "Lukács debate".

He arrives at Budapest on 1st August 1945 and becomes a Member of Parliament. Later he takes up the chair of Aesthetics and Philosophy of Culture at Budapest University and becomes a Member of the Praesidium of the Hungarian Academy of Sciences.

In addition to a second edition of *Irástudók felelössége*—which stands at the centre of cultural-ideological discussions in Hungary—he publishes two volumes of essays in Hungarian: *Balzac, Stendhal, Zola* and *József Attila költészete* (The Poetry of Attila József). His first German volume is *Fortschritt und Reaktion in der deutschen Literatur* (Progress and Reaction in German Literature), published in Berlin by Aufbau-Verlag who remain his publishers until his deportation in 1956.

1946/49
He starts a feverish literary activity in Hungarian newspapers and periodicals, and before the "Lukács debate" begins he publishes numerous volumes of essays of varying size in many languages (twenty volumes and pamphlets in Hungarian alone).

He founds the cultural periodical *Forum* in 1946 and remains its spiritual (though not formal) director until its suppression—as a result of the Lukács debate —in 1950.

In 1946 he takes part in the discussions of the "Rencontres internationales de Genève" with a lecture on "La vision aristocratique et démocratique du monde" and he is involved in a sharp confrontation with Karl Jaspers, his friend during the years of study at Heidelberg.

The project of writing *Die Zerstörung der Vernunft* is conceived in this period (with several partial studies published in various volumes between 1946/49) but realized only in the aftermath of the Lukács debate, thanks to the forced retirement from literary-political activity, and published simultaneously in Hungarian and German in 1954.

He travels extensively both in Eastern Europe and in the West, including France, Austria, Switzerland and Italy.

In December 1947 he delivers a lecture in Milan, at the international conference of Marxist philosophers, in "The Tasks of Marxist Philosophy in the New Democracy".

At the beginning of 1949 he takes part in the discussions at the Hegel Conference in Paris dedicated to "Les nouveaux problèmes de la recherche hégélienne".

On his trips to Paris he meets several French philosophers, both militants of the party (Emile Bottigelli, Jean Desanti, Roger Garaudy, Henri Lefèbvre) and outside it (Lucien Goldmann, Jean Hyppolite, Maurice Merleau-Ponty), as well as numerous other intellectuals in the field of art and literature. He becomes a founding member of the World Council for Peace in 1948 and participates in its activities—involving numerous journeys abroad—between 1948/56. (He resigns in 1957).

In 1948 he is awarded the Kossuth Prize.

1949/52

1949 is labelled by Rákosi as "the year of turn-about": a radical change in policy, coinciding in cultural policy with the "Lukács debate" and in politics with the Rajk trial.

The attacks on Lukács are opened by his old supporter turned adversary: László Rudas, who publishes a long article full of abuse in the party's theoretical organ *Társadalmi Szemle* (Social Review), followed by attacks in the daily press and in virtually every periodical in the country. He is accused of "revisionism", "right-wing deviationism", "cosmo-politanism", of having "calumnied Lenin", of being objectively a "servant of imperialism" etc., etc. Márton Horváth, second in command in the field of culture to Révai only and a member of the Politbuio, joins in the attacks with an article of sharp condemnation.

Events take an even more serious turn when Fadyeev publishes a violent attack in *Pravda*, foreshadowing the possibility of severe measures of punishment.

The immediate object of attack is constituted by two volumes of essays written between 1945/48: *Irodalom és demokrácia* (Literature and Democracy) and *Uj magyar kultúráért* (For New Hungarian Culture), published in 1947 and 1948, but the issues of the 'thirties ("Proletcult", "schematism", "socialist realism", etc.) as well as of the 'twenties ("Blum Theses" and *History and Class Consciousness*) come to the fore.

Lukács publishes a self-critical article, but it is declared to be "merely formal" by József Révai: the party's top theoretician and unquestionable leader in cultural-political matters. Despite the sharpness of Révai's attack, Lukács always thinks of his intervention as a positive one in the sense that it virtually puts an end to further attacks (the condemnation he receives from József Darvas a few months later at the Writers' Congress in 1951 does not matter in the least, notwithstanding Darvas' rank as Minister of Culture) and prevents the arrest he feared at the time when Fadyeev and *Pravda* became involved in the matter.

In 1952 Brecht and Lukács bury the old expressionist hatchet and renew their friendship. Between 1952 and Brecht's death in August 1956 Lukács always visits Brecht whenever he goes to Berlin.

In 1952/53 the novelist Tibor Déry is repeatedly attacked and Lukács takes his part in the debates.

In November 1952 Lukács completes *Die Zerstörung der Vernunft* (The Destruction of Reason): a monumental analysis of 150 years of German philosophical developments in relation to dialectics and irrationalism.

1953/55

The period of "thaw" greatly improves Lukács' situation and his books start to appear again.

To celebrate his seventieth birthday Aufbau-Verlag publishes a volume in 1955—*Georg Lukács zum siebzigsten Geburtstag*—with the participation of many distinguished people, including Ernst Bloch and Thomas Mann. He is also elected corresponding member of the German Academy of Sciences in Berlin.

In Hungary he receives the Kossuth Prize for his life work in 1955.

In France Merleau-Ponty publishes *Les aventures de la dialectique* in 1955: a work that puts into the centre of philosophical debate Lukács' *History and Class Consciousness* and has a great impact on subsequent philosophical development, including Sartre's *Critique de la raison dialectique*.

1956

In the aftermath of the 20th Congress many taboos are swept aside and the old cultural and political debates are reopened. Lukács takes an active part in these debates and he presides over the philosophy debate held at the Petöfi Circle on 15 June.

He travels extensively (Germany, Austria, Italy, Sweden) and lectures on the theme of the volume later published under the title: *The Meaning of Contemporary Realism*.

Another famous lecture from this period is entitled *The Struggle of Progress and Reaction in Contemporary Culture*. It is delivered at the Party Academy in Budapest on June 28.

Towards the end of June a discussion takes place at the Institute for the History of the Working Class Movement on the "Blum Theses" with his participation.

In the summer of 1956 he founds a new periodical: *Eszmélet* ("Prise de conscience") with Aurél Bernáth, Tibor Déry, Gyula Illés, Zoltán Kodály, and István Mészáros as its editor. After Rákosi's departure from politics the periodical receives the go-ahead from the Ministry of Culture.

On October 24 he becomes a member of the enlarged Central Committee and Minister of Culture in Imre Nagy's Government.

On November 4th he takes refuge, together with other political figures, at the Yugoslav embassy. He is deported to Rumania when they leave the embassy.

1957/62
On April 10th 1957 he returns from deportation to his home at Budapest.

He refuses to join the newly constituted party. (Contrary to widely held belief he was never expelled, nor refused readmission.)

Attacks on Lukács are reopened with increased vehemence, and led in the first place by his former pupil József Szigeti: Deputy Minister of Culture at the time.

Lukács' Department at the University is closed and thus he is deprived of all contact with students.

The attacks continue for several years—in Hungary, Germany, Russia, and other East European countries —and in 1960 Aufbau-Verlag, Berlin, publish a 340 page long volume entitled *Georg Lukács und der Revisionismus.*

Lukács publishes in Italy his *Prolegomeni a un' estetica marxista* (Editori Riuniti) and *Il significato attuale del realismo critico* (i.e. "The Meaning of

Contemporary realism", Einaudi) in 1957. In the
same year he also publishes in Italy a *Postscript* to
"My Road to Marxism" in which he formulates a
sharp critique of Stalinism and its continued survival. He carries on the same discourse in 1962 in
an open *Letter to Alberto Carocci*, Editor of *Nuovi
Argomenti*.

Luchterhand-Verlag begins in 1962 the publication of his collected works with *Die Zerstörung der
Vernunft*.

Lukács' principal work of the period—1957-62—
is his monumental *Aesthetics*: completed at the end
of 1962 and published the following year in two
massive volumes, entitled *Die Eigenart des Ästhetichen*
(The Specificity of the Aesthetic).

1963
After the completion of his *Aesthetics* he begins
writing his *Ontology of Social Being* with great
enthusiasm. The work is cruelly interrupted by the
sudden death of his wife on April 28. (The *Aesthetics*
carries a moving dedication to Gertrud Bortstieber.)

For several months he struggles against the desire
to commit suicide. His loss is recorded in an essay on
Mozart and Lessing—Gertrud's favourites—*Minna
von Barnhelm*: perhaps the most beautiful writing of
Lukács' entire work.

1964/68

He takes up work again on his *Ontology of Social Being* but never succeeds in completing it to his own satisfaction.

In September 1966 he holds an important series of conversations with Wolfgang Abendroth, Hans Heinz Holz, and Leo Kofler, published subsequently under the title: *Gespräche mit Georg Lukács* (Rowohlt 1967, edited by Theo Pinkus).

In 1967 he writes an extensive new Introduction to a volume of early political writings which includes *History and Class Consciousness*. The latter is reissued both in Italian and in German in 1968.

He gives a series of interviews and writes several articles on the problems of "destalinization" and bureaucratization. They culminate in a most important study, dedicated to a rigorous examination of the question of socialist democracy in the period of transition. Written in 1968, and completed after the occupation of Czechoslovakia against which Lukács strongly protested, this major study remains unpublished to date. (Only a small section appeared in a volume by Lukács on Lenin, published in Hungary on the occasion of the Lenin centenary.)

In 1968 Lukács' early political writings appear in Germany in "pirate editions" and they figure heavily in the debates of the extra-parliamentary opposition all over Europe as well as in America.

1969/70

He is elected Hon. Doctor at Zagreb University in 1969.

Towards the end of 1969 he starts writing his *Prolegomena to a Social Ontology*.

In the same period he rejoins the party.

In 1970 he becomes a Honorary Doctor of Ghent University and also receives the Goethe Prize of the city of Frankfurt am Main.

In December the doctors discover that he is at the terminal phase of cancer. He is told that he has only a short time to live. He continues work with greater intensity than ever.

1971

He works on the *Prolegomena* until a few days before his death. At the same time he fills many pages with autobiographical notes.

He continues organizing an international action of intellectuals to save Angela Davis.

His last public appearance is at the Bartók festivities: he delivers a lecture dedicated to the memory of the great contemporary only a few weeks before his death.

He dies at Budapest, on the 4th June 1971. A few days later he is buried at the Kerepesi cemetery, in a plot reserved for the great figures of the Hungarian socialist movement.

BIBLIOGRAPHY

A) *Works of Lukács*

1902
"Theatre" (in Hungarian), *Magyar Szalon,* Nov. and Dec.

1903
"Theatre" (in Hung.), *Magyar Szalon,* Jan., Febr., March,
    April, May and July.
"Hermann Bang"; "The New Hauptmann" (in Hung.), both
    in: *Jövendö.*

1906
"The Form of the Drama" (in Hung.), *Szerda.*
"Thoughts on Henrik Ibsen" (in Hung.), *Huszadik Század.*

1907
"Gauguin" (in Hung.), *Huszadik Század*.

1908
"Novalis"; "Rudolf Kassner"; "Stefan George"; "Der Weg ins Freie: Arthur Schnitzler's Novel"; "Books on Ibsen" (in Hung.), all in: *Nyugat*.
"The Novellas of Lajos Biró"; "Thália Rediviva"; "New Hungarian Poets" (in Hung.), all in: *Huszadik Század*.

1909
"Richard Beer-Hoffmann"; "Notes on Margit Szélpál"; "Thomas Mann's New Novel"; "Anzengruber" (in Hung.), all in: *Nyugat*.
"The Novellas of Dániel Jób"; "On August Strindberg's Six-tieth Birthday"; "Doctor Margit Szélpál"; "The Possibility of Social Drama"; "New Hungarian Lyric Poetry"; "The Novellas of Zsigmond Móricz" (in Hung.), all in: *Huszadik Század*.
"The Form of the Drama" (in Hung.), *Budapesti Szemle*.
A dráma formája (The Form of the Drama), Franklin: Budapest.

BIBLIOGRAPHY

1910

"The Roads Have Divided"; "Sören Kierkegaard and Regine Olsen"; "Lajos Fülep on Nietzsche"; "On the So-called Obscurity: Answer to Mihály Babits" (in Hung.), all in: *Nyugat.*

"Aesthetic Culture"; "Charles-Louis Philippe"; "They Are Afraid of Health" (in Hung.), all in: *Renaissance.*

"Die Gedichte von Béla Balázs", *Pester Lloyd.*

Megjegyzések az irodalomtörténet elméletéhez (Observations on the Theory of Literary History), Franklin: Budapest.

A lélek és a formák (The Soul and the Forms), Franklin: Budapest.

1911

"Shakespeare and Modern Drama" (in Hung.), *Magyar Shakespeare–Társaság.*

"'The Novellas of Pontopiddan" (in Hung.), *Aurora.*

"On Poverty of Soul"; "Metaphysics of the Tragedy"; "Leopold Ziegler"; "Wilhelm Dilthey"; "Jewish Mysticism" (in Hung.), all in: *Szellem.*

"Über Sehnsucht und Form", *Die neue Rundschau.*

"Metaphysik der Tragödie", *Logos.*

"Brunhild (Paul Ernst)", *Die Schaubühne.*

"Leo Popper. Ein Nachruf", *Pester Lloyd.*

A modern dráma fejlödésének története (History of the Development of Modern Drama), 2 vols., Franklin: Budapest.

Die Seele und die Formen, Egon Fleischel & Co.: Berlin.

BIBLIOGRAPHY

1912
"Von der Armut am Geiste". Ein Gespräch und ein Brief",
Neue Blätter.

1913
"A Few Words on the Form of the Drama: to Mihály Babits";
"Béla Balázs: The Last Day" (in Hung.), both in: *Nyugat.*
"Der Dramatiker des neuen Ungarn", *Pester Lloyd.*
"Gedanken zu einer Ästhetik des Kinos", *Frankfurter Zeitung*
Esztétikai kultúra (Aesthetic Culture), Athenaeum: Budapest.

1914
"Zur Soziologie des modernen Dramas"; "Th. G. Masaryk:
  Zur russischen Geschichte und Religionsphilosophie", both
  in: *Archiv für Sozialwissenschaft und Sozialpolitik.*

1915
"Zum Wesen und zur Methode der Kultursoziologie"; On "W.
  Solovjeff: Ausgewählte Werke Bd. I."; On "B. Croce:
  Zur Theorie und Geschichte der Historiographie"; On
  "M.-L. Gothein: Geschichte der Gartenkunst", all in:
  Archiv für Sozialwissenschaft und Sozialpolitik.

BIBLIOGRAPHY

1916

"Ariadne auf Naxos", *Paul Ernst zu seinem 50. Geburtstag.*

On "W. Solovieff: Ausgewählte Werke Bd. II.", *Archiv für Sozialwissenschaft und Sozialpolitik.*

"Die Theorie des Romans", *Zeitschrift für Ästhetik und Allgemeine Kunstwissenschaft.*

"Observations on Béla Balázs' New Poems" (in Hung.), *Nyugat.*

1917

"On Rózsi Forgács" (in Hung.), *Nyugat.*

"Die Subjekt-Objekt Beziehung in der Ästhetik", *Logos.*

1918

"The Debate Between Conservative and Progressive Idealism"; "Ferenc Molnár's Andor" (in Hung.), both in: *Huszadik Század.*

"The Relationship Between Subject and Object in Aesthetics" (in Hung.), *Athenaeum.*

"Georg Simmel. Ein Nachruf", *Pester Lloyd.*

"Emil Lask. Ein Nachruf", *Kant-Studien.*

"Bolshevism as Moral Problem" (in Hung.), *Szabad Gondolat.*

Balázs Béla és akiknek nem kell (Béla Balázs and His Adversaries), Kner: Gyoma.

1919

"The Effective Possession of Culture" (in Hung.), *Fáklya.*

"Freedom of the Press and Capitalism"; "Clarification"; "What Is Revolutionary Action?"; "Speech at the First Congress of the KMP"; "Speech at the Congress of the National Confederation of Young Workers" (in Hung.), all in: *Vörös Ujság.*

"Tactics of the Victorious Proletariat"; "The True Unity" (in Hung.) both in: *Népszava.*

"Order of the Law and Violence", "The Question of Intellectual Leadership and 'Intellectual Workers' "; "Old Culture and New Culture"; "The Changing Function of Historical Materialism" (in Hung.), all in: *Internationale.*

"The Role of Morality in Communist Production" (in Hung.); *Szociális Termelés.*

Preface to Podách–Vértes: *The Direction of Social Development,* Lantos: Budapest.

"Bericht über die Rede auf dem Kongress des ungarischen Landesverbandes der Jungarbeiter in Budapest, August 1919", *Freie Jugend.*

Taktika és Ethika (Tactics and Ethics), Közoktatásügy Népbiztosság: Budapest.

1920

"Zur Organisationsfrage der Intellektuellen"; "Die neueste überwindung des Marxismus: Kritik an O. Spengler: Untergang des Abendlandes"; "Zur Frage des Parlamentarismus"; "Organisationsfragen der dritten Internationale"; "Klassenbewusstsein"; "Die moralische Sendung der kommunistischen Partei"; "Kapitalistische Blockade, proletarischer Boykott";

BIBLIOGRAPHY

"Opportunismus und Putschismus"; Legalität und Illegalität"; "Die Krise des Syndikalismus in Italien"; "Kassel und Halle"; "Alte und neue Kultur"; "Der Parteitag der Kommunistischen Partei Deutschlands", all in: *Kommunismus.*

"The Social Hinterland of White Terror"; "Crises of Government"; "Why The Hungarian Dictatorship of the Proletariat Has Not Been Defeated?"; "The Freedom Struggle of the Colonies"; "Self-Criticism"; "Boycott and Boycott"; "Ottó Korvin"; "Revolution and Counter-revolution"; "The Unity of the German Proletariat"; "Mass Strike and Workers' Councils"; "Spoiled Festivities"; "The Crisis of the Italian Revolution"; "The Communist Party and Political Workers' Councils in Germany"; "White Terror and the Independents"; "Where Do We Stand?"; "Attempt at Consolidation"; "Danger Zone"; "On the 100th Anniversary of Engels' Birth"; "Who is Speculating?"; "Trade Unions on a Revolutionary Road"; "General Bodone" (in Hung.), all in: *Proletár.*

Die Theorie des Romans. Ein geschichtsphilosophischer Versuch über die Formen der grossen Epik, Paul Cassirer: Berlin.

1921
"Two = Nought"; "The Balance Sheet of the Prussian Elections"; "Ultimatum of the Entente—The Stock Exchange Is Quiet"; "German Crisis"; "The Hungarian Crisis Becomes Permanent"; "Before Tempest"; "Paul Levi"; "German Ultimatum and World Crisis"; "The Congress of Görlitz" (in Hung.), all in: *Proletár.*

"Rosa Luxemburg als Marxist"; "Ukrainischer Nationalbolschewismus"; "Vor dem dritten Kongress", all in: *Kommunismus.*

"Weltreaktion und Weltrevolution (Vortrag auf der 2. Südostkonferenz der Kommunistischen Jugend-Internationale in Wien", *Flugschriften der Jugend-Internationale.*

"Zur Frage de Bildungsarbeit"; "Partei und Jugendbewegung

BIBLIOGRAPHY

in Ungarn"; "Zur Frage von 'Partei und Jugend' ", all in:
Jugend-Internationale.
"Spontaneität der Massen, Aktivität der Partei"; "Organisa-
torische Fragen der revolutionären Initiative", both in: *Die
Internationale.*
"Diskussionsbeitrag auf dem III. Weltkongress der Kom-
munistischen Internationale" (13th Session, 2 July 1921),
*Protokoll des III. Kongresses der Kommunistischen Inter-
nationale, Moskau, 22. Juni bis 12 Juli 1921.*
Preface to Rosa Luxemburg: *Tömegsztrájk* (Mass Strike, in
Hung.), Verlag der Arbeiter-Buchhandlung: Wien.

1922
"Noch einmal Illusionspolitik", in: Ladislaus Rudas,
*Abenteurer—und Liquidatorentum. Die Politik Béla Kuns
und die Krise der K. P. U.*, Wien.
"Die K. P. R. und die proletarische Revolution", *Die Rote
Fahne.*

1923
*Geschichte und Klassenbewusstsein. Studien über marxistische
Dialektik*, Malik-Verlag: Berlin.

1924
"Lenin", *Das Forum.*
"Lassalle als Theoretiker der VSDP"; "Der Triumph Bern-
steins. Bemerkungen über die Festschriften zum 70. Geburts-

tag Karl Kautskys", both in: *Die Internationale.*
On "M. Adler: Das Soziologische in Kants Erkenntniskritik",
 *Internationale Presse-Korrespondenz für Politik, Wirtschaft
 und Arbeiterbewegung.*
Lenin. Studie über den Zusammenhang seiner Gedanken,
 Malik-Verlag: Berlin.

1925
"Lassalle's New Followers"; "Jókai"; "Morocco–Syria–China";
 "Why Did Comrade Rákosi Go to Hungary?" (in Hung.),
 all in: *Új Március.*
On "N. Bucharin: Theorie des historischen Materialismus";
 On "K. A. Wittfogel: Die Wissenschaft der bürgerlichen
 Gesellschaft"; "Die neue Ausgabe von Lassalles Briefen", all
 in: *Archiv für die Geschichte des Sozialismus und der
 Arbeiterbewegung.*

1926
"Moses Hess und die Probleme der idealistischen Dialektik";
 On "W. I. Lenin: Ausgewählte Werke"; On "Unter dem
 Banner des Marxismus, I. Jahrgang, Heft 1-2", all in:
 *Archiv für die Geschichte des Sozialismus und der Arbeiter-
 bewegung.*
"Lajos Kassák", (in Hung.), *Új Március.*
"Der Nelson-Bund", *Die Internationale.*
Moses Hess und die Probleme der idealistischen Dialektik,
 Verlag Hirschfeld: Leipzig.

1927

"Eine Marxkritik im Dienste des Trotzkismus, Rez. von Max Eastman: Marx, Lenin and the Science of Revolution", *Die Internationale.*

"The Impact of October in the East" (in Hung.), *Új Március.*

"The Handshake of Two Ghosts Over a Grave" (in Hung.), *100%.*

1928

"Peasant Novels: János Kodolányi"; "On the 10th Anniversary of Plekhanov's Death" (in Hung.), both in: *100%.*

"Jenö Landler: Fight Against Death"; "Counter-revolutionary Forces under the Hungarian Proletarian Dictatorship"; "The Trend of Industrial Development and Class Conscious Workers' Politics" (in Hung.), all in: *Új Március.*

On "Edgar Zilsel: Die Entstehung des Geniebegriffs"; On "Othmar Spann: Kategorienlehre"; On "Carl Schmitt: Politische Romantik"; On "Jakob Baxa: Gesellschaft und Staat im Spiegel deutscher Romantik"; On "Robert Michels: Zur Soziologie des Parteiwesens in der modernen Demokratie", all in: *Archiv für die Geschichte des Sozialismus und der Arbeiterbewegung.*

1929

On "O. Rühle: Geschichte der Revolutionen Europas", *Archiv für die Geschichte des Sozialismus und der Arbeiterbewegung.*

"Blum: Declaration" (in Hung.), *Új Március.*

BIBLIOGRAPHY

1931

"Die Fabrik im Walde"; "Über den Dostojewski-Nachlass"; "Neue russische Belletristik", all in: *Moskauer Rundschau*.

"Shaws Bekenntnis zur Sowjetunion"; "Willi Bredels Romane", both in: *Die Linkskurve*.

"Über das Schlagwort Liberalismus und Marxismus", *Der Rote Aufbau*.

1932

"Goethe's World View" (in Hung.), *Valóság*.

"Gegen die Spontaneitätstheorie in der Literatur"; "Tendenz oder Parteilichkeit"; "Der faschisierte Goethe"; "Reportage oder Gestaltung. Kritische Bemerkungen anlässlich des Romans von Ottwalt"; "Aus der Not eine Tugend"; "Gerhart Hauptmann", all in: *Die Linkskurve*.

"Goethe und die Dialektik", *Der Marxist*.

"Zur Frage der Satire", *Internationale Literatur*.

"Kritik der Literaturtheorie Lassalles", *Der Rote Aufbau*.

1933

"Die Sickingendebatte zwischen Marx-Engels und Lassalle"; "Mein Weg zu Marx", both in: *Internationale Literatur*.

BIBLIOGRAPHY

1934
" 'Grösse und Verfall' des Expressionismus", *Internationale Literatur.*

1935
"Hölderlins Hyperion"; "Nietzsche als Vorläufer der faschistischen Ästhetik", both in: *Internationale Literatur.*

1936
"Friedrich Engels als Literaturhistoriker und Literaturkritiker"; "Thomas Mann über das literarische Erbe"; "Der Befreier"; "Zum Verfassunngsentwurf der UdSSR"; "Erzählen oder Beschreiben?" all in: *Internationale Literatur.*
"Die intellektuelle Physiognomie der künstlerischen Gestalten"; *Das Wort.*

1937
"Arnold Zweig: Erziehung vor Verdun"; "Schillers Theorie der modernen Literatur"; " 'Die menschliche Komödie' des vorrevolutionären Russlands"; "Die Tragödie Heinrich von Kleist"; "Heinrich Heine als nationaler Dichter", all in: *Internationale Literatur.*
"Der faschisierte und der wirkliche Georg Büchner", *Das Wort.*
"Über bürgerlichen Realismus", '*U*'.
"Eine klassische Darstellung des dialektischen Materialismus:

Engels' Anti-Dühring"; "Ludwig Feuerbachs Erbe"; "Zum 20. Jahrestag der Oktober-Revolution", all in: *Deutsche Zentral-Zeitung.*

1938

"Maxim Gorki—der proletarische Humanist"; "Über Johannes R. Becher"; "Julius Háys Drama 'Haben' ", all in: *Deutsche Zentral-Zeitung.*

"Über Tolstoi"; "Diderot und die Probleme der Theorie des Realismus"; "Der Briefwechsel zwischen Schiller und Goethe", all in: *Deutsche Zeitung.*

"Der Kampf zwischen Liberalismus und Demokratie im Spiegel des historischen Romans der deutschen Antifaschisten"; "Marx und das Problem des ideologischen Verfalls"; "Leo Tolstoi und die Entwicklung des Realismus", all in: *Internationale Literatur.*

"Das Ideal des harmonischen Menschen in der bürgerlichen Ästhetik"; "Es geht um den Realismus"; On "Heinrich Mann: Die Jugend des König Henri Quatre"; "Unveröffentliches aus Tolstois Nachlass"; "Der plebeische Humanismus in der Ästhetik Tolstois", all in: *Das Wort.*

1939

"Ady, Great Poet of the Hungarian Tragedy"; "The Responsibility of Intellectuals: Marginal Notes to a Volume of Gyula Illyés"; "On Socialist Realism"; "Lost Illusions"; "Observations on 19th Century Russian Revolutionary Criticism"; "How Was Stalin's Book: 'Foundations of Leninism' Received in Capitalist Countries When It Appeared?" (in Hung.), all in: *Új Hang.*

"Zu Andor Gábors 'Ungarischem Inferno' "; "Wilhelm Meisters

BIBLIOGRAPHY

Lehrjahre"; "Arnold Zweigs Romanzyklus über den imperialistischen Krieg"; "Über die demokratische Jugendentwicklung Franz Mehrings"; "Ein Briefwechsel zwischen Anna Seghers und Georg Lukács"; "Gottfried Keller"; "Schriftsteller und Kritiker", all in: *Internationale Literatur*.

1940

"Volkstribun oder Bürokrat"; "Eichendorff"; "Wilhelm Raabe", all in: *Internationale Literatur*.

"Fight or Capitalution: Notes on Some Issues of *Szép Szó*"; On "Balzac: Peasants"; "The Hundred Year Old Zola"; "Again and Again: What is the Hungarian?"; "Two Plays by Gyula Háy"; "Hungarian Democratic Historiography and the History of Modern Democracies"; "Gorki's Epic Art" (in Hung.), all in: *Új Hang*.

Gottfried Keller, Staatsverlag der nationalen Minderheiten der UdSSR: Kiew.

1941

"Aktualität und Flucht"; "Johannes R. Bechers 'Abschied' "; "Faust-Studien I: Zur Entstehungsgeschichte"; "Faust-Studien II: Das Drama der Menschengattung", all in: *Internationale Literatur*.

"Heine und die ideologische Vorbereitung der 48er Revolution", *Kommunistische Internationale*.

"Gorky's Artistic Method"; "Prologue or Epilogue?"; "The Confessions of Mihály Babits" (in Hung.), all in: *Új Hang*.

BIBLIOGRAPHY

1942

"Die verbrannte Poesie"; "Das innere Licht ist die trübste Beleuchtungsart", both in: *Internationale Literatur*.

1943

"Über Preussentum"; "Der Igel"; "Adam Scharrer: Der Landsknecht"; "Der deutsche Faschismus und Hegel"; "Der deutsche Faschismus und Nietzsche", all in: *Internationale Literatur*.

1944

"Schicksalswende", *Internationale Literatur*.
Irástudók felelössége (The Responsibility of Intellectuals), Idegennyelvü Irodalmi Kiadó: Moscow.

1945

"Hungarian Intellectuals and Democracy"; "The Road of Democracy I: The Example of the Great French Revolution"; "The Road of Democracy II: The Contradictions of the Great French Revolution"; "Forum Club"; "Black Christmases", (in Hung.), all in: *Szabad Nép*.
"The Galavyov Family"; "Puskin: The Captain's Daughter" (in Hung.) both in: *Új Szó*.

BIBLIOGRAPHY

"Leo Tolstoy and Western Literature" (in Hung.), *Magyarok.*
"Der Rassenwahn als Feind des menschlichen Fortschritts",
    Aufbau.
"Die deutsche Literatur im Zeitalter des Imperialismus. Abriss
    ihrer Hauptströmungen"; "Auf dem Suche nach dem Bürger";
    "Fortschritt und Reaktion in der deutschen Literatur", all
    in: *Internationale Literatur.*
Irástudók felelőssége (The Responsibility of Intellectuals, en-
    larged ed.), Szikra: Budapest.
József Attila költészete (The Poetry of Attila József), Szikra:
    Budapest.

1946
"Lenin"; "Cultural Problems of the Hungarian Democracy";
"God, Emperor, Peasant: Gyula Háy's Play at the National
    Theatre"; "Gorky: On the 10th Anniversary of His Death";
    "Béla Fogarasi: Marxism and Logic"; "Marxism and the
    Bourgeois Intelligentsia"; "Interview with G. Lukács on His
    Journey to Geneva" (in Hung.), all in: *Szabad Nép.*
"Saltykov-Shchedrin"; "Pushkin"; "Ostrovsky" (in Hung.), all
    in *Új Szó.*
" 'The Crisis of Democracy'—Or Its Right-wing Critique?";
    "On Prussianhood", (in Hung.), both in: *Valóság.*
"Ferenc Baumgarten: A Memorial Lecture" (in Hung.),
    Irodalom-Tudomány.
"Gorky's Work" (in Hung.), *Utunk.*
"Settling Accounts with the Past" (in Hung.), *Új Magyarország.*
"Democracy and Culture"; "Pál Justus: The Road to Social-
    ism"; "Literature and Democracy"; "Zsigmond Móricz's
    Call"; "Socialism"; "Jenő Osvát's Writings"; "Géza
    Bárcsai: The Struggle of Hungarian Science against
    German Imperialism"; "Sándor Szalai: Social Reality and
    Social Science" (in Hung.), all in: *Társadalmi Szemle.*
"The Unity of Hungarian Literature"; "*Újhold*"; "The First
    Issue of *Válasz*" (in Hung.), all in: *Fórum.*
"Working Class Movement and Workers' Culture" (in Hung.),
    Munkásszinpad.

BIBLIOGRAPHY

"On Dezsö Szabó" (in Hung.), *Szivárvány*.

"On Russian Science" (in Hung.), *Embernevelés*.

"Deutsche Soziologie vor dem ersten Weltkrieg"; "Die deutsche Soziologie zwischen dem ersten und dem zweiten Weltkrieg", both in: *Aufbau*.

"Die geistige Krise der modernen Gesellschaft", *Neuer Vorwärts*.

"L'esprit européen devant le marxisme" (Lecture at the 'Rencontres Internationales de Genève'); "Deux philosophies de l'Europe: marxisme et existentialisme", both in: *La Nef*.

Lenin és a kultúra kérdései (Lenin and the Problems of Culture), Magyar-Szovjet Müvelödési Társaság: Budapest.

Népi irók a mérlegen (Populist Writers under Scrutiny), Szikra: Budapest.

Az újabb német irodalom rövid története (a Short History of Modern German Literature), Athenaeum: Budapest.

Nagy orosz realisták (Great Russian Realists), Szikra: Budapest.

Goethe és kora (Goethe and His Age), Hungária: Budapest.

1947

"Against Old and New Legends"; "Kassák at Sixty"; "Free or Directed Art?"; "To the Margins of a Bad Novel"; "Noémi Ferenczy"; "The Centenary of Toldi"; "For an Unprejudiced Conception of Literature"; "Observations on a Literary Debate"; "Hungarian Theories of Abstract Art"; "Changed World Outlook"; "Ady Does Not Parley" (in Hung.), all in: *Fórum*.

"Lenin's Epistemology and the Problems of Modern Philosophy"; "The World Outlook of Capitalism—in Reformist Mirror"; "The Crisis of Bourgeois Philosophy" (in Hung.), all in: *Társadalmi Szemle*.

"Discussions on Communist Aesthetics"; "On Topical Issues of Hungarian Literature"; "Opening Speech at the Exhibition of the Attila József Sculpture Competition" (in Hung.), all in: *Szabad Nép*.

"Culture for the People of the Countryside" (in Hung.), *Irodalmi Szemle*.

BIBLIOGRAPHY

"Diary of a Journey" (in Hung.), *Nagyvilág*.

"Ferenc Fejtö's Heine" (in Hung.), *Csillag*.

Goethe und seine Zeit, Francke: Bern.

Irodalom és demokrácia (Literature and Democracy), Szikra: Budapest.

A történelmi regény (The Historical Novel), Hungária: Budapest.

A marxi esztétika alapjai (Outlines of a Marxist Aesthetics), Szikra: Budapest.

A 'giccsröl' és a 'proletkultról' (On 'Kitsch' and 'Proletcult'), Szikra: Budapest.

A polgár nyomában: a hetvenéves Thomas Mann (In Search of Bourgeois Man: Thomas Mann at Seventy), Hungária: Budapest.

A polgári filozófia válsága (The Crisis of Bourgeois Philosophy), Hungária: Budapest.

1948

"Comrade György Lukács on the Conference of Marxist Philosophers in Milan"; "What Is Despair Good For?"; "Cultural Revolution and People's Democracy"; "On Optimist Literature"; "Planned Economy and Marxist World View"; "Leo Tolstoy: On the 120th Anniversary of His Birth"; "Letter to Young Hungarian Writers"; "Against 'Western' Ideology"; "The Failure of Capitalist Culture"; "The Revolt of Parasitism"; "The Revision of the History of Hungarian Literature"; "The Hungarian Communist Party and Culture" (in Hung.), all in: *Szabad Nép*.

"Letter to Andor Németh on Tibor Déry's Novel"; "Márai's Novel"; "Fascism and Democracy"; "Some Problems of Marxist Aesthetics"; "Thirty Years of the Communist Party in Hungary" (in Hung.), all in: *Fórum*.

"Past and Present of Populist Literature" (in Hung.), *Valóság*.

"Revision of the History of Literature and the Teaching of Literature" (in Hung.), *Embernevelés*.

"People's Democracy and Literature" (in Hung.), *Népszava*.

"Marxist Aesthetics"; "The True Freedom of Art and Science"; "Correspondence with Tibor Déry on Optimism"; "The

BIBLIOGRAPHY

Defence of Peace and the Responsibility of Intellectuals" (in Hung.), all in: *Csillag.*

"On the Front of Philosophy"; "Károly Kerényi: Daughters of the Sun" (in Hung.), both in: *Társadalmi Szemle.*

"The Problems of Change"; "On the Ethos of Work of the New University" (in Hung.), both in: *Fiatal Magyarország.*

"Les tâches de la philosophie marxiste dans la nouvelle démocratie", *Studi Filosofici.*

"Im Elfenbeinturm der Unverbindlichkeit"; "Was draussen geschrieben wurde"; "Der wahre Wert", all in: *Sonntag.*

"Die funktionelle Problematik der sowjetischen Literatur", *Die Fähre.*

"Aktivität statt Verzweiflung", *Tägliche Rundschau.*

"Die Intelligenz am Scheidewege", *Österreichisches Tagebuch.*

"Stanislavsky's International Significance", in: *The National Theatre to Stanislavsky's Memory* (in Hung.), Budapest.

Der junge Hegel. Über die Beziehungen von Dialektik und Ökonomie, Europa Verlag: Zürich & Wien.

Essays über Realismus, Aufbau-Verlag: Berlin.

Schicksalswende. Beiträge zu einer neuen deutschen Ideologie, Aufbau-Verlag: Berlin.

Karl Marx und Friedrich Engels als Literaturhistoriker, Aufbau-Verlag: Berlin.

Existentialisme ou marxisme, Nagel: Paris.

A Realizmus problémái (The Problems of Realism), Athenaeum: Budapest.

Új magyar kultúráért (For a New Hungarian Culture), Szikra: Budapest.

A marxista filozófia feladatai az új demokráciában (The Tasks of Marxist Philosophy in the New Democracy), Budapest Székesfövárosi Irodalmi Intézet: Budapest.

1949

"On the Anniversary of Jenö Landler's Death", "The Tasks of Marxist Critique" (in Hung.), both in: *Szabad Nép.*

"Our Goethe" (in Hung.), *Irodalomtörténet.*

171

BIBLIOGRAPHY

"From Wroclaw to Paris: Interview with Professor Lukács" (in Hung.), *Fiatal Magyarország*.

"The First Veritable Book-day" (in Hung.), *Irodalmi Szemle*.

"The Depiction of the Enemy: Virta's 'Solitude' "; "Pushkin's Place in World Literature"; " 'Quiet Flows the Don': The Epos of the Civil War in Cossack Country" (in Hung.), all in: *Fórum*.

"Criticism and Self-criticism" (in Hung.), *Társadalmi Szemle*.

"Les nouveaux problèmes de la recherche hégélienne", *Bulletin de la Société Française de Philosophie*.

"Pourquoi on s'intéresse à la littérature allemande?", *La Tribune des Nations*.

Ady Endre (Endre Ady), Szikra: Budapest.

1950

"Herzen: Selected Philosophical Essays"; "Conclusions from the Literary Debate"; (in Hung.), both in: *Társadalmi Szemle*.

"Heroes of the Great Patriotic War" (in Hung.), *Csillag*.

"Contribution to the Discussion at the Annual General Meeting of the Hungarian Academy of Science" (in Hung.), *Akadémiai Értesitö*.

"Egon Erwin Kisch, der Meister der Reportage", *Heute und Morgen*.

1951

"Contribution to the Discussion at the Peace Meeting of the Hungarian Academy of Science"; "Literature and Art as Superstructure"; "Contribution to the Discussion at the Annual General Meeting of the Hungarian Academy of Science" (in Hung.), all in: *Akadémiai Értesitö*.

BIBLIOGRAPHY

"Plekhanov: On the Development of the Monist Conception of History"; "The Berlin Session of the World Council for Peace"; "The Vienna Session of the World Council for Peace" (in Hung.), all in: *Társadalmi Szemle.*

"Speech at the Writers' Congress"; "The Smith of the New Man"; "Fadyeyev: The Nineteen" (in Hung.), all in: *Csillag.*

"Maxim Gorky's Literary Essays" (in Hung.), *Irodalmi Ujság.*

"Lessing: On the 170th Anniversary of His Death"; "Don Quixote"; "Gogol: The Inspector"; "Saltykov-Shchedrin: Story of a Town; Abroad" (in Hung.), all in: *Szabad Nép.*

"Sprachwissenschaft und Literatur", *Aufbau.*

"Der alte Fontane"; "Wozu braucht die Bourgeoisie die Verzweiflung?", both in: *Sinn und Form.*

Deutsche Realisten des 19. Jahrhunderts, Aufbau-Verlag: Berlin.

1952

"Gruss an Arnold Zweig", *Sinn und Form.*

"Zum Problem des Schematismus", *Schriftsteller.*

"Cultural Policy of the Councils' Republic"; "We Are Defending Also the Cause of Culture against Capitalist Barbarism"; "Contribution to the Session on Attila József's Poetry" (in Hung.), all in *Irodalmi Ujság.*

"Strength and Perspective of the World Peace Movement" (in Hung.), *Szabad Nép.*

"Observations on the Problems and Tasks of Art History" (in Hung.), *Szabad Müvészet.*

"The Foundation of Irrationalism between Two Revolutions: 1789-1848"; "Walter A. Kaufmann: Nietzsche, Philosoph, Psychologe und Antichrist" (in Hung.), both in: *Filozófiai Évkönyv.*

"On Imre Madách" (in Hung.), *A Magyar Tudományos Akadémia I. Osztály Közleményei.*

"Ludwig Feuerbach's Selected Philosophical Writings"; "Extraordinary Session of the World Peace Council in Berlin" (in Hung.), both in: *Társadalmi Szemle.*

BIBLIOGRAPHY

"Present Situation and New Problems of the Fight against Schematism"; "Gogol" (in Hung.), both in: *Csillag*.

"Contribution to the Literary Debate Held at the Lecturers' Central Bureau of the MKP", in: *Vita irodalmunk helyzetéröl* (Debate on the State of Our Literature), Szikra: Budapest.

"Introduction to Hegel's Aesthetics", in Hegel: *Esztétikai elöadások* (Lectures on Aesthetics), Akadémiai Kiadó: Budapest.

"Introduction to Chernyshevsky's Aesthetics", in: Chernyshevsky: *Esztétikai Tanulmányok* (Studies on Aesthetics), Akadémiai Kiadó: Budapest.

Balzac und der französische Realismus, Aufbau-Verlag: Berlin.

Der russische Realismus in der Weltliteratur, vermehrte und verbesserte Auflage, Aufbau-Verlag: Berlin.

1953

"Schellings Irrationalismus"; "Karl Marx und Friedrich Theodor Vischer"; "Kierkegaard", all in: *Deutsche Zeitschrift für Philosophie*.

"Dostojewskij"; "Tolstoy und die westliche Literatur", both in: *Heute und Morgen*.

"Marx und Engels über dramaturgische Fragen"; "Tschernischewskij und die Tragödie", both in: *Aufbau*.

"Die Werke von Marx und Engels in Ungarn", *Börsenblatt für den deutschen Buchhandel*.

"Einführung in die ästhetischen Schriften von Marx und Engels"; "Hegels Ästhetik", both in: *Sinn und Form*.

"Contribution to the Discussion at the Annual General Meeting of the Hungarian Academy of Science"; "Speech at the Closing Session of the General Meeting of the Hungarian Academy of Science" (in Hung.), both in: *Akadémiai Értesitö*.

"The Peace Congress of Nations" (in Hung.), *Társadalmi Szemle*.

"Stalin: Economic Problems of Socialism in the Soviet Union" (in Hung.), *Egyetemek és Föiskolák békemozgalma*.

174

BIBLIOGRAPHY

"Sketch to a Portrait of Andor Gábor" (in Hung.), *Irodalmi Ujság.*
Skizze einer Geschichte der neueren deutschen Literatur, Aufbau-Verlag: Berlin.
Adalékok az esztétika történetéhez (Contributions to a History of Aesthetics), Akadémiai Kiadó: Budapest.

1954
"Contribution to the Discussion on Béla Fogarasi's Lecture: Theoretical and Practical Problems of the Classification of the Sciences"; "Contribution to the Discussion at the Annual General Meeting of the Hungarian Academy of Science" (in Hung.), both in: *A Magyar Tudományos Akadémia II. Osztály Közleményei.*
"Tibor Déry at Sixty" (in Hung.), *Irodalmi Ujság.*
"Irrationalist Ideology of the Post-War Period" (in Hung.), *Társadalmi Szemle.*
"Kunst und objektive Wahrheit"; "Zur philosophischen Entwicklung des jungen Marx: 1840-1844"; "Die Frage der Besonderheit in der klassischen Philosophie", all in: *Deutsche Zeitschrift für Philosophie.*
"Wendung zum Volk", in: *Lion Feuchtwanger zum 70. Geburtstag,* Aufbau-Verlag: Berlin.
Az ész trónfosztása. Az irracionalista filozófia kritikája (The Destruction of Reason. A Critique of Irrationalist Philosophy), Akadémiai Kiadó: Budapest.
Die Zerstörung der Vernunft, Aufbau-Verlag: Berlin.
Beiträge zur Geschichte der Ästhetik, Aufbau-Verlag: Berlin.

1955
"Speech at the Opening Session of the Hungarian Academy of Science, 1 April 1955" (in Hung.), *Akadémiai Értesitö.*

BIBLIOGRAPHY

"The Problem of Aesthetic Reflection" (in Hung.), *A Magyar Tudományos Akadémia II. Osztály Közleményei.*

"Madách's Tragedy" (in Hung.), *Szabad Nép.*

"On the 50th Anniversary of the Foundation of the Thália Company"; "Political Partisanship and Poetic Fulfilment" (in Hung.), both in: *Csillag.*

"Thomas Mann und das heutige öffentliche Leben", *Ungarische Rundschau.*

"Das Besondere im Lichte des dialektischen Materialismus"; "Der Verfall des historischen Bewusstseins", both in: *Deutsche Zeitschrift für Philosophie.*

"Das Spielerische und seine Hintergründe. Fragmentarische Bemerkungen zum ersten Teil der 'Bekenntnisse des Hochstaplers Felix Krull' ", *Aufbau.*

"Der letzte grosse Vertreter des kritischen Realismus"; "Briefwechsel mit Thomas Mann", both in: *Sinn und Form.*

"Das ästhetische Problem des Besonderen in der Aufklärung und bei Goethe", in: *Ernst Bloch zum 70. Geburtstag,* Verlag der Wissenschaften: Berlin.

"Introduction" to Tibor Déry: *A ló meg az öregasszony. Válogatott elbeszélések* (The Horse and the Old Woman. Selected Short Stories), Magvetö: Budapest.

Der historische Roman, Aufbau-Verlag: Berlin.

Probleme des Realismus, Aufbau-Verlag: Berlin.

1956

"Das Besondere als zentrale Kategorie der Ästhetik"; "Zur Konkretisierung der Besonderheit als Kategorie der Ästhetik", both in: *Deutsche Zeitschrift für Philosophie.*

"Es lebe die verbotene KPD"; "Der Kampf des Fortschritts und der Reaktion in der heutingen Kultur", both in: *Aufbau.*

"Das Problem der Perspektive", *Beiträge zur Gegenwartsliteratur.*

"A haladás és reakció harca a mai kultúrában" (in Hung.), *Társadalmi Szemle.*

"Extracts from the 'Blum Theses' " (in Hung.), *Párttörténeti*

176

BIBLIOGRAPHY

Közlemények.

"Interview with Gy. Lukács on the Free Discussions of Artistic and Philosophical Trends, on the Recent Debates about Socialist Realism and on His Plans"; "Radio Message of Professor György Lukács, Minister of Culture, to the Hungarian Youth" (in Hung.), both in: *Szabad Nép.*

"Extracts from György Lukács' Speech at the Philosophy Debate of the Petöfi Circle" (in Hung.), *Filozófiai Értesitö.*

"György Lukács' Presidential Address at the Opening Session of the Congress of Literary Historians", in: *A realizmus kérdései a magyar irodalomban* (The Problems of Realism in Hungarian Literature), Akadémiai Kiadó: Budapest.

"Lettre à la rédaction des *Cahiers du Communisme*", in: *Mésaventures de l'Anti-Marxisme*, Editions Sociales: Paris.

1957

"Une protestation de G. Lukács", *Arguments.*

A különösség mint esztétikai kategória (On Particularity as a Category of Aesthetics), Akadémiai Kiadó: Budapest.

Il significato attuale del realismo critico, Einaudi: Torino.

Prolegomeni a un'estetica marxista, Editori Riuniti: Roma.

1958

"La mia via al marxismo: Postscriptum 1957", *Nuovi Argomenti.*

"G. Lukács e I. Mészáros: Sui problemi estetici del cinematografo", *Cinema Nuovo.*

Wider den missverstandenen Realismus, Claasen: Hamburg.

BIBLIOGRAPHY

1960

"Une déclaration de G. Lukács, concernant l'édition française d'*Histoire et Conscience de Classe*", *Arguments*.

Histoire et Conscience de Classe. Essais de Dialectique Marxiste, Les Editions de Minuit: Paris.

Geschichte und Klassenbewusstsein. Studien über marxistische Dialektik, *Kleine Revolutionäre Bibliothek No. 9* (Dupl.), Universität: Hamburg.

1961

"Diavolo azzurro o diavolo giallo?" (Answer to U. Barbaro: Lukács, il film e la tècnica), *Cinema Nuovo*.

Schriften zur Literatursoziologie, ausgewählt und eingeleitet vom Peter Ludz, Luchterhand: Neuwied.

1962

"Lettera a Alberto Carocci', *Nuovi Argomenti*.

"Contribution to the Discussion at the Annual General Meeting of the Hungarian Academy of Science", *Akadémiai Értesitõ*.

Die Zerstörung der Vernunft, mit einem neuen Vorwort, *Werke Bd. 9*, Luchterhand: Neuwied.

1963

"Zur Debatte zwischen China und der Sowjetunion. Theoretisch-philosophische Bemerkungen", *Forum*.

178

BIBLIOGRAPHY

Die Eigenart des Ästhetischen, Werke Bd. 11 & 12, Luchterhand: Neuwied.
*Die Theorie des Romans. Ein geschichtsphilosophischer Versuch
über die Formen der grossen Epik,* mit einem neuen Vorwort,
Luchterhand: Neuwied.

1964

"Probleme der kulturellen Koexistenz", *Forum.*
"Gespräch mit Georg Lukács: Über Literatur-Probleme in
Ost und West" (Interview with Antonin Liehm), *Tagebuch.*
"Theatre and Environment", *The Times Literary Supplement.*
*Probleme des Realismus II., Der russische Realismus in der
Weltliteratur, Werke Bd. 5,* Luchterhand: *Neuwied.*
Deutsche Literatur in zwei Jahrhunderten, Werke Bd. 7,
Luchterhand: Neuwied.

1965

"Theodor Pinkus: Georg Lukács zwischen Revisionismus und
Dogmatismus, Gespräch mit dem ungarischen Philosophen
und Literaturwissenschaftler", *Die Weltwoche.*
"Günther Specovius: Gespräch mit dem marxistischen Literatur-
kritiker in Budapest", *Sonntagsblatt.*
"Hannsjakob Stehle: Plädoyer für den Marxismus, Gespräch
mit dem Philosophen Georg Lukács", *Die Zeit.*
"Gespräche über marxistische Theorie, Arbeiterdemokratie und
Sartre mit Georg Lukács", *express-international.*
"On the Question of Romanticism", *The New Hungarian
Quarterly.*
Preface to Guido Aristarco: *Il dissolvimento della ragione.
Discorso sul cinema,* Feltrinelli: Milano.
Probleme des Realismus III., Der historische Roman, Werke

BIBLIOGRAPHY

Bd. 6, Luchterhand: Neuwied.

Der junge Marx. Seine philosophische Entwicklung von 1840 bis 1844, Neske: Pfullingen.

1966

"Technology and Social Relations", *New Left Review.*

"Interview with Lukács" (in Hung., Branko Peitsch), *Hid* (extracts in: *Die Welt*).

"Realismo socialista de hoy", *Revista de Occidente.*

Von Nietzsche bis Hitler oder der Irrationalismus in der Deutschen Politik, Fischer-Bücherei: Frankfurt.

1967

"Der grosse Oktober 1917 und die heutige Literatur", in: *ad lectores 5,* Luchterhand: Neuwied.

"Conversation with György Lukács" (in Hung.), *Irodalmi Múzeum.*

"Lo scrittore a piede libero" (Interview with G. L., Naim Kattan), *L'Espresso.*

Der junge Hegel. Über die Beziehungen von Dialektik und Ökonomie, Werke Bd. 8, Luchterhand: Neuwied.

Gespräche mit Georg Lukács (Hans Heinz Holz, Leo Kofler, Wolfgand Abendroth; ed. by Theo Pinkus), Rowohlt: Reinbek.

Über die Besonderheit als Kategorie der Ästhetik, Luchterhand: Neuwied.

BIBLIOGRAPHY

1968

"Alle Dogmatiker sind Defaitisten", *Forum.*

"Some Problems of Peaceful Co-existence" (in Hung.), *Kortárs.*

"An Interview with Gy. Lukács" (P. Rényi and P. Pándi), *The New Hungarian Quarterly.*

"The Cinema Has a Vanguard Role in Present-Day Hungarian Culture" (an Interview with Yvette Biró, in Hung.), *Filmkultúra.*

"Il marxismo nella coesistenza", *Il Contemporaneo.*

Frühschriften II., Geschichte und Klassenbewusstsein, Werke Bd., 2, Luchterhand: Neuwied.

1969

"My Road to Hungarian Culture"; "The New Economic Course and Socialist Culture" (in Hung.), both in: *Kortárs.*

"Hungarian Literature—World Literature: an Interview with György Lukács" (Miklós Almási, in Hung.), *Kritika.*

"The Ontological Foundations of Human Thought and Activity"; "My Marxist Development: 1918-1930" (in Hung.), both in: *Magyar Filozófiai Szemle.*

"Reminiscences of Mária and György Lukács on Béla Bartók" (in Hung.), *Muzsika.*

"Il comunismo si sblocca solo se rompe per sempre con Stalin" (Interview with Mario Pirani), *Il Giorno.*

"Può mutare davvero qualcosa?—Colloquio con György Lukács", *L'Espresso.*

"On the Responsibility of the Intellectuals", *Telos.*

"Die Deutschen—eine Nation der Spätentwickler? Gespräch mit Adelbert Reif", *Neues Forum.*

"Die ontologische Grundlagen des menschlichen Denkens und Handelns", in: *ad lectores 8,* Luchterhand: Neuwied.

Az esztétikum sajátossága (The Particularity of the Aesthetic, shortened Edition), Magvetö: Budapest.

Világirodalom. Válogatott világirodalmi tanulmányok I. II. (Selected Essays on World Literature), Gondolat Kiadó: Budapest.

Probleme der Ästhetik, Werke Bd. 10, Luchterhand: Neuwied

BIBLIOGRAPHY

1970
"Goethe's Example" (in Hung.), *Kortárs.*
"The Twin Crises" (an Interview), *New Left Review.*
"The Old Culture and the New Culture", *Telos.*
"È possibile la rivoluzione?"; "Napoleone e l'aritmetica";
"Do'vè oggi lo spirito del mondo?" (Interviews with G.
Lukács), all in: *L'Espresso.*
"Nach Hegel nichts neues", *Neues Forum.*
"Georg Lukács über Futurologie", *Futurum.*
"Lenin und die Fragen der Übergangsperiode"; "Zur Organ-
isationsfrage der Intellektuellen"; "Alte Kultur und neue
Kultur"; "Zur Verleihung des Goethepreises", all in:
Goethepreis '70, Luchterhand: Neuwied.
Lenin (5 essays, in Hung.), Magvetö: Budapest.
Magyar irodalom—magyar kultúra. Válogatott tanulmányok
(Hungarian Literature— Hungarian Culture. Selected
Essays), Gondolat Kiadó: Budapest.
Müvészet és társadalom (Art and Society), Gondolat Kiadó:
Budapest.

1971
"Labour" (in Hung.), *Valóság.*
"A Conversation with György Lukács" (András Kovács, in
Hung.), *Új Irás.*
"A Morning with György Lukács" (Áron Tóbiás, in Hung.),
Múzsák.
"The Dialectic of Labor", *Telos.*
"An Interview with G. Lukács: On His Life and Work", *New
Left Review.*
"Quando Breznev non ci sarà più" (an Interview), *L'Espresso.*
Utam Marxhoz I.-II. (My Road to Marx. Selected Essays),
Gondolat Kiadó: Budapest.
*Probleme des Realismus I., Essays über Realismus, Werke Bd.
4*, Luchterhand: Neuwied.
*Zur Ontologie des gesellschaftlichen Seins. Hegels falsche und
echte Ontologie*, Luchterhand: Neuwied.

BIBLIOGRAPHY

B) Books of Lukács in English

Studies in European Realism (transl. by Edith Bone; Hillway:
London 1950; reissued by Merlin Press: London 1972).
   Preface (1948).
   Balzac: The Peasants (1934).
   Balzac: Lost Illusions (1935).
   Balzac and Stendhal (1935).
   The Zola Centenary (1940).
   The International Significance of Russian Democratic
      Literary Criticism (1939).
   Tolstoy and the Development of Realism (1936).
   The Human Comedy of Pre-Revolutionary Russia (1936).
   Leo Tolstoy and Western European Literature (1944).

The Historical Novel (transl. by Hannah and Stanley Mitchell,
Merlin Press: London 1962).
   Preface to the English Edition (1960).
   Foreword (1937).
   I. THE CLASSICAL FORM OF THE HISTORICAL NOVEL.
     1. Social and Historical Conditions for the Rise of the
        Historical Novel.
     2. Sir Walter Scott.
     3. The Classical Historical Novel in Struggle with Romanti-
        cism.
   II. HISTORICAL NOVEL AND HISTORICAL DRAMA.
     1. Facts of Life Underlying the Division between Epic and
        Drama.
     2. The Peculiarity of Dramatic Characterization.
     3. The Problem of Public Character.
     4. The Portrayal of Collision in Epic and Drama.
     5. A Sketch of the Development of Historicism in Drama
        and Dramaturgy.
   III. THE HISTORICAL NOVEL AND THE CRISIS OF BOURGEOIS
        REALISM.
     1. Changes in the Conception of History after the Revolu-
        tion of 1848.
     2. Making Private, Modernization and Exoticism.
     3. The Naturalism of the Plebeian Opposition.
     4. Conrad Ferdinand Meyer and the New Type of Historical
        Novel.
     5. The General Tendencies of Decadence and the Establish-

The Meaning of Contemporary Realism (U.S. edition: *Realism in Our Time*; trans. by John and Necke Mander; Merlin Press: London 1963).
  Preface to the English Edition (1962).
  Preface to the German Edition (1957).
  Introduction.
  The Ideology of Modernism.
  Franz Kafka or Thomas Mann?
  Critical Realism and Socialist Realism.

Essays on Thomas Mann (transl. by Stanley Mitchell; Merlin Press: London 1964).
  Foreword (1963).
  In Search of Bourgeois Man (1945).
  The Tragedy of Modern Art (1948).
  The Playful Style (1955).
  "Royal Highness" (1909).
  Thomas Mann on the Literary Heritage (1936).
  The Last Great Critical Realist (1955).

Goethe and His Age (transl. by Robert Anchor; Merlin Press: London 1968).

BIBLIOGRAPHY

Preface (1947).
"Minna von Barnhelm" (1963).
"The Sorrows of Young Werther" (1936).
"Wilhelm Meister's Apprenticeship" (1936).
The Correspondence between Schiller and Goethe (1934).
Schiller's Theory of Modern Literature (1935).
Hölderlin's "Hyperion" (1934).
"Faust" Studies (1940).
1. Origins.
2. The Drama of the Human Species.
3. Faust and Mephistopheles.
4. The Tragedy of Gretchen.
5. Problems of Style: The End of the "Artistic Period".

Solzhenitsyn (transl. by W. D. Graf; Merlin Press: London
1970).
"One Day in the Life of Ivan Denisovich" (1964).
Solzhenitsyn's Novels (1969).

Writer and Critic (transl. by Arthur Kahn; Merlin Press:
London 1970).
Preface (1970).
Art and Objective Truth (1954).
Marx and Engels on Aesthetics (1948).
The Ideal of the Harmonious Man in Bourgeois Aesthetics
(1938).
Healthy or Sick Art? (1952).
Narrate or Describe? (1936).
The Intellectual Physiognomy in Characterization (1936).
The Writer and the Critic (1939).
Pushkin's Place in World Literature (1949).

BIBLIOGRAPHY

Lenin. A Study on the Unity of his Thought (transl. by
  Nicholas Jacobs; N L B: London 1970).
  Foreword (1924).
  1. The Actuality of the Revolution.
  2. The Proletariat as the Leading Class.
  3. The Vanguard Party of the Proletariat.
  4. Imperialism: World War and Civil War.
  5. The State as Weapon.
  6. Revolutionary *Realpolitik*.
  Postscript (1967).

History and Class Consciousness. Studies in Marxist Dialectics
  (transl. by Rodney Livingstone; Merlin Press: London 1971).
  Preface to the New Edition (1967).
  Preface (1922).
  What is Orthodox Marxism? (1919).
  The Marxism of Rosa Luxemburg (1921).
  Class Consciousness (1920).
  Reification and the Consciousness of the Proletariat
  (1921/22).
      1. The Phenomenon of Reification.
      2. The Antinomies of Bourgeois Thought.
      3. The Standpoint of the Proletariat.
  The Changing Function of Historical Materialism (1919).
  Legality and Illegality (1920).
  Critical Observations on Rosa Luxemburg's "Critique of the
  Russian Revolution" (1922).
  Towards a Methodology of the Problem of Organization
  (1922).

*The Theory of the Novel. A Historico-Philosophical Essay on
  the Forms of Great Epic Literature* (transl. by Anna
  Bostock; Merlin Press: London 1971.
  Preface (1962).

IN PREPARATION:

Political Writings, 1919-26. The Question of Parliamentarism and Other Essays (N L B: London 1972).

The Soul and the Forms (Merlin Press: London 1973).

The Young Hegel (Merlin Press: London 1973).

The Destruction of Reason (Merlin Press: London 1974).

BIBLIOGRAPHY

C) Works on Lukács

Adorno, T. W., "Erpresste Versöhnung", *Der Monat*, Nov. 1958. *Negative Dialektik*, Frankfurt 1966.

Althaus, H., *Georg Lukács oder Bürgerlichkeit als Vorschule einer marxistischen Ästhetik*, Bern-München 1962.

Alvarez, F., "Sobre 'Significación actual del realismo critico' ", *Revista Mexicana de Literatura*, 1964 (n. 3/4).
"En defensa de Lukács", *La cultura en México* (suppl. of *Siempre!*), 13 May 1964.

Amodio, L., "Der alte Lukács", *Ragionamenti*, 1956 (n. 5/6).
"Tra Lenin e Luxemburg. Commentario al periodo 'estremistico' di G. Lukács: 1919-21", *Il Corpo*, 1967 (n. 5).
"Il passaggio di Lukács al leninismo"; "Ancora su Lukács. Risposta a T. Perlini", both in: *Nuova Corrente*, 1969 (n. 48).

Amoruso, V., "Lukács e i problemi del realismo", *Aut-Aut*, 1958 (n. 47).

Arblaster, A., "A Masterpiece of Marxist Criticism", *Tribune*, 23 Febr. 1962.

Arvon, H., *Georges Lukács. Le Front populaire en littérature*, Paris 1968.

Asor Rosa, A., "Il giovane Lukács: teorico dell'arte borghese", *Contropiano*, 1968 (n. 1).

Axelos, K., Preface to G. L. *Histoire et conscience de classe*, Paris 1960.

Badaloni, N., "La rivolta contro Hegel e il ritorno di Engels", *Rinascita*, Jan. 1970.

Bahr, E., *Georg Lukács*, Berlin 1970.

Bango, E., "La conscience de classe chez G. Lukács", *Documentation sur l'Europe Centrale*, 1966 (n. 4).

BIBLIOGRAPHY

Barbaro, U., "Lukács, il film e la tecnica", *L'Unità*, 22 Jan.
Logos, 1912.

Baxandall, L., *Marxism and Aesthetics*, New York 1968.

Bedeschi, G., "Critica della società e critica della scienza in
'Storia e coscienza di classe' di György Lukács", *Angelus
Novus*, 1968 (n. 12/13). *Introduzione a Lukács*, Bari 1970.

Bense, M., "Der Fall Georg Lukács", *Aufklärung*, 1959.
"Georg Lukács zum 70. Geburtstag", *Augenblick*, 1955 (n. 3).

Benseler, F. (ed.), *Festschrift zum 80. Geburtstag von Georg
Lukács*, Neuwied 1965. (Contributions by: W. Abendroth,
G. Anders, E. Ansermet, G. Aristarco, R. Assunto, B.
Baczko, F. Benseler, C. Cases, T. Déry, K. Farner, E. Fischer,
O. Flake, G. K. Freyer, L. Goldmann, R. Gutiérrez Girardot,
A. Heller, R. Hochhuth, W. Hofmann, H. H. Holz, L.
Kolakowski, J. Lindsay, L. Löwenthal, P. Ludz, H. Mayer,
I. Mészáros, L. Mittner, H. Pross, P. Rossi, J. Rühle, V.
Santoli, A. Schaff, R. W. Schnell, G. Steiner, B. Szabolcsi,
W. Szilasi, C. Vasoli, J. Vogt, A. West).

Berger, J., *Toward Reality. Essays in Seeing*, London 1962.

Birnbaum, N., *Toward a Critical Sociology*, Oxford University
Press 1971.

Bloch, E., "Aktualität und Utopie. Zu Lukács' Geschichte und
Klassenbewusstsein" (1923), in: *Philosophische Aufsätze*,
Frankfurt 1969.
"Discussionen über Expressionismus" (1938), in: *Erbschaft
dieser Zeit*, Frankfurt 1962.

Borkenau, F., "Der Fall Georg Lukács", *Rheinischer Merkur*,
26 Apr. 1957.

Brecht, B., *Schriften zur Literatur und Kunst* Vol II., Berlin-
Weimar 1966.

Breines, P., "Introduction to Lukács: The Old Culture and
the New Culture", *Telos*, Spring 1970.
Recension of Books on Lukács, *Telos*, Summer 1970.

Breton, S., "L'irrationalisme selon G. Lukács", in: *La crise
de la raison dans la pensée contemporaine*, Paris-Bruges 1960.

Burgum, E. B., "The Historical Novel in the Hands of Georg
Lukács", *Science and Society*, Winter 1966.

BIBLIOGRAPHY

Carbonara, C., *L'estetica del particolare di G. Lukács*, Napoli 1960. *L'estetica del particolare di G. Lukács e G. Della Volpe*, Messina 1961.

Cases, C., "Lo scoiattolo e l'elefante: Ritratto di G. Lukács", *Il Contemporaneo*, 25 Apr. 1956.

  Marxismo e neopositivismo, Torino 1958.

  "Le idee politiche di Havemann e di Lukács", *Quaderni Piacentini*, 1966 (n. 27).

  "A proposito del saggio di Lukács: Vecchia Kultur e Nuova Kultur", *Quaderni Piacentini*, 1971 (n. 43).

Cassa, M., "La dialettica 'incommensurabile' di György Lukács", *Drammaturgia*, July 1957.

Cassano, F., " 'Reificazione' e 'disalienazione' in G. Lukács", *Rinascita*, 1969 (n. 39).

Cazalis, S., "Hacia una estética dialéctica", *Revolución*, 28 Jan. 1964.

Cerutti, F., "Lukács, Croce e la sociologia", *Il Corpo*, 1967 (n. 5).

Chiarini, P., *Letteratura e società*, Bari 1959.

  "Brecht e Lukács. A proposito del concetto di realismo" *Società*, 1961 (n. 1).

Chiodi, P., *Sartre e il marxismo*, Milano 1965.

Colletti, L., "Intervento sui problemi del realismo", *Il Contemporaneo*, 1959 (n. 11). *Il marxismo e Hegel*, Bari 1969.

Coutinho, C., N., *Literatura e Humanismo*, Rio de Janeiro 1967.

Croce, B., On "G. L.: Goethe und seine Zeit", *Quaderni della Critica*, July 1949.

Daix, P., "Lukács et nous", *Les Lettres Françaises*, 6 March 1968.

Davie, D., "Beyond the Boudoir", *The Guardian*, 23 Febr. 1962.

Deborin, A., "Lukács und seine Kritik des Marxismus". *Arbeiterliteratur*, 1924 (n. 10).

Della Volpe, G., *Critica del gusto*, Milano 1960 & 1964.

BIBLIOGRAPHY

Demetz, P., "Zwischen Klassik und Bolschewismus", *Merkur.* June 1958.

"The Uses of Lukács", *The Yale Review*, 1964/65.

Déry, T., "György Lukács", *The New Hungarian Quarterly,* Autumn 1971.

Deutscher, I., "Georg Lukács and 'Critical Realism' ", *The Listener*, 3 Nov. 1966.

Dévérité, J. (Leo Kofler), *Der Fall Lukács*, Köln 1952.

Diersen, I., "Zu G. Lukács' Konzeption der deutschen Literatur im Zeitalter des Imperialismus", *Weimarer Beiträge. Zeitschrift für deutsche Literaturgeschichte*, 1958.

Elsberg, J., "Zu den falschen Anschauungen von G. Lukács", *Die Presse der Sowjetunion*, 1958 (n. 99).

Eörsi, I., "György Lukács and the Theory of Lyric Poetry"; "György Lukács: Fanatic of Reality" both in: *The New Hungarian Quarterly*, Summer 1965, Winter 1971.

Esslin, M., "The Karl Marx of Aesthetics", *The Spectator*, 2 March 1962. "Solzhenitsyn and Lukács", *Encounter*, 1971.

Faucci, D., "Intorno all'estetica di Lukács", *Rivista di Estetica.* 1967.

Fejtö, F., "G. Lukács entre le dogmatisme et le révisionnisme" *Esprit*, 1961.

Fetscher, I., "Das Verhältnis des Marxismus zu Hegel" *Marxismus-Studien 3*, 1960.

Finale, C., "Lukács tra ideologia e utopia", *Tempo Presente* 1964 (n. 6).

Finetti, U., "Lukács e Della Volpe e i problemi critici del film", *Cinema Nuovo*, 1968 (n. 185).

Fischer, E., *Kunst und Koexistenz*, Reinbek 1966. *Erinnerungen und Reflexionen*, Reinbek, 1969.

Flores Olea, V., "Lukács y el problema del arte", in: *Marxisme*

191

y democracia socialista, México 1969.

Politica y dialéctica, México 1964.

Fortini, F., "G. Lukács, Thomas Mann e la tragedia dell'arte moderna", *Il Ponte*, 1956 (n. 5).

Introduction to G. L., *L'anima e le forme*, Milano 1963.

"Lukács in Italia"; "Lukács giovane", both in: *Verifica dei poteri*, Milano 1965.

Fröschner, G., *Die Herausbildung und Entwicklung der geschichtsphilosophischen Anschauungen von G. Lukács*, Berlin 1965.

Furter, P., "La pensée de G. Lukács en France", *Revue de théologie et de Philosophie*, 1961.

Gabel, J., *La fausse conscience: essai sur la réification*, Paris 1962.

Gallas, H., "Ausarbeitung einer marxistischen Literaturtheorie in BPRS und die Rolle von G. Lukács", *Alternative*, 1969 (n. 67/8).

Garaudy, R., *D'un réalisme sans rivages*, Paris 1963.

Garcia Ponce, J., "Sobre el realismo crítico de Lukács", *Revista Mexicana de Cultura*, 1964 (n. 3/4).

Georg Lukács zum 70. Geburtstag, Berlin 1955.

(Contributions by: A. Abusch, A. Baumgarten, J. R. Becher, J. D. Bernal, E. Bloch, E. Bottigelli, G. Caspar, A. Cornu, G. Cwojdrak, H. Eisler, F. Erpenbeck, K. Farner, E. Fischer, B. Fogarasi, W. Harich, W. Herzfelde, H. H. Holz, H. Iwand, J. Jahn, W. Janka, H. Kamnitzer, R. Karst, J. Kuczynski, W. Langhoff, H. Lefèbvre, J. Lindsay, P. F. Linke, L. Magon, Th. Mann, W. Markov, H. L. Markschies, H. Mayer, O. Morf, C. Morgan, P. Nenni, R. Pascal, A. Schaff, A. Seghers, W. Steinitz, K. Stern, V. Stern, T. de Vries, A. Zweig).

Gerratana, V., "Lukács e i problemi del realismo", *Società*, 1953.

Gisselbrecht, A., "Les aventures du 'marxisme occidental'", *La Nouvelle Critique*, 1955 (n. 6/7).

Goldmann, L., *Sciences humaines et philosophie*, Paris 1952.

MARX'S THEORY OF ALIENATION

Much of the discussion of Marxism today revolves round the problems of alienation.

The author shows how the concept was central to Marx's whole development of a critique of society, from the early manuscripts to *Capital*, and counters the view that there is a philosophically-oriented "young Marx" and a "mature Marx" concerned with "economic determinism". The significance of the Marxian theory of alienation is assessed in its proper perspectives : in the development and historical impact of Marx's work as a whole.

In his approach to the subject, Dr Mészáros shows the same wide-ranging insights as his former teacher, Georg Lukács. Historical material, from a broad spectrum of experience in the fields of philosophy and economics as well as sociology and literature, is integrated in the framework of a systematic structural and conceptual analysis of the complex issues involved. Written in the first place to satisfy the need of students for a comprehensive treatment, this book, by its emphasis on the practical significance of alienation in the 20th century, is essential reading for all those interested in the development of socialist theory.

BIBLIOGRAPHY

Le dieu caché, Paris 1956.

Recherches dialectiques, Paris 1959.

"L'esthétique du jeune Lukács"; "Marx, Lukács, Girard et la sociologie du roman", both in: *Médiations*, 1961.

"Introduction aux premier écrits de Georges Lukács", *Les Temps Modernes*, Aug. 1962.

Pour une sociologie du roman, Paris, 1964.

Gouldner, A. W., "History and Class Consciousness", *The New York Times Book Review*, 18 July 1971.

Guérin, D., "Sartre, Lukács et . . . la Gironde", *Les Temps Modernes*, 1957.

Guiducci, A., *Dallo zdanovismo allo strutturalismo*, Milano 1967.

Harrington, M., "A Marxist Approach to Art", *The New International*, Spring 1956.

"Georg Lukács", *Anvil*, 1957 (n. 1).

"Marxist Literary Critics", *Commonwealth*, 11 Dec. 1959.

Hauser, A., *The Social History of Art*, London 1951.

Heimann, E., "*Vernunftsglaube und Religion in der modernen Gesellschaft*, Tübingen 1955.

Heise, W., "Zur ideologisch-kritischen Konzeption von G. Lukács", *Weimarer Beiträge. Zeitschrift für deutsche Literaturgeschichte*, 1958.

"Zu einigen Problemen der literaturtheoretischen Konzeption von G. Lukács", *Junge Kunst*, 1958 (n. 7).

Heller, A., "Lukács' Aesthetic", *The New Hungarian Quarterly*, Winter 1966.

Hill, A. G., "Marxist Aesthetics", *The Critical Survey*, Autumn 1963.

Hitchens, C., "The Project of the Whole Man", *The Times*, 11 March 1971.

Holthusen, H. E., "G. Lukács und die moderne Literatur", *Neue Zürcher Zeitung*, 1958 (n. 300).

Horst, K. A., "Literaturkritik von Links. Anmerkungen zu W. Benjamin und G. Lukács", *Wort und Wahrheit*, 1956 (n. 7).

Hyppolite, J., "Aliénation et objectivation: à propos du livre de Lukács sur la jeunesse de Hegel", *Études Germaniques*, 1951 (n. 2).

Kaufmann, H., "Wider den sozialistischen Realismus. Lukács' Konzeption eines 'dritten' Weges", *Neue Deutsche Literatur*, 1959 (n. 9/10).

Kautsky, K., "Lukács: Geschichte und Klassenbewusstsein", *Die Gesellschaft*, June 1924.

Kettle, A., "Lukács on the Novels of Solzhenitsyn", *Morning Star*, 25 Febr. 1971.

Kettler, D., *Marxismus und Kultur. Mannheim und Lukács in den ungarischen Revolutionen 1918/19*, Neuwied 1967.

Koch, H. (ed.), *Georg Lukács und der Revisionismus*, Berlin 1960.

Koch, M., "Politik, Literaturwissenschaft und die Position von G. Lukács"; "Theorie und Politik bei G. Lukács", both in: *Einheit*, 1957 (n. 7 & 8).

Kofler, L. (S. Warynski), *Die Wissenschaft von der Geselschaft*, Bern 1944.
Geschichte und Dialektik, Hamburg 1955.

Kolakowski, L., "Lukács' Other Marx", *Cambridge Review*, 28 Jan. 1972.

Konder, L., *Os Marxistas e a Arte*, Rio de Janeiro 1967.

Korsch, K., *Marxismus und Philosophie*, Leipzig 1932.

Kovács, A., "Interview with Lukács on Lenin and on the Student Movements", *Cambridge Review*, 28 Jan. 1972.

Lefèbvre, H., "La notion de totalité", *Cahiers Internationaux de Sociologie*, 1955. "La philosophie de G. Lukács", *Conférence à l'Institut Hongrois de Paris*, 8 June 1955.

Lichtheim, G., "An Intellectual Disaster", *Encounter*, May

1963.
The Concept of Ideology and Other Essays, New York 1967.
Lukács, London, 1970.
Lizalde, E., "Lukács, perseguidor perseguido", *La Cultura en México*, 29 Apr. 1964.
Ludz, P., "Marxismus und Literatur—Eine kritische Einführung in das Werk von Georg Lukács", Pref. to *G. Lukács: Schriften zur Literatursoziologie*, Neuwied 1961.
Lübbe, H., "Zur marxistischen Auslegung Hegels", *Philosophische Rundschau*, 1954/55 (n. 1/2).
Lukes, S., "A Veteran Marxist", *The Observer*, 14 Febr. 1971.

MacIntyre, A., "Marxist Mask and Romantic Face: Lukács on Thomas Mann", *Encounter*, Apr. 1965.
Mandel, E., *La formation de la pensée économique de Karl Marx*, Paris 1967.
Mann, Th., *Die Betrachtungen eines unpolitischen*, Berlin 1920.
Mannheim, K., *Ideology and Utopia*, London 1936.
Marck, S., "Neukritizistische und neuhegelsche Auffassung der marxistischen Dialektik", *Die Gesellschaft*, 1924 (n. 8).
"Dialektisches Denken in der Philosophie der Gegenwart", *Logos*, 1926.
Die Dialektik in der Philosophie der Gegenwart I. II., Tübingen 1929 & 1931.
Der Neuhumanismus als politische Philosophie, Zürich 1938.
"Georg Lukács und der Irrationalismus", *Die Neue Gessellschaft*, 1955 (n. 5).
Marcuse, H., "Transzendentaler Marxismus?"; "Neue Quellen zur Grundlegung des historischen Materialismus", both in: *Die Gesellschaft*, 1930 & 1932.
Maslow, V., "Georg Lukács and the Unconscious", *The Journal of Aesthetics and Art Criticism*, 1963.
"Lukács' Man-Centred Aesthetics", *Philosophy and Phenomenological Research*, 1967.
Mayer, H., *Bertolt Brecht und die Tradition*, Pfullingen 1961.
"Zwei Ansichten über Georg Lukács", in: *Zur deutschen Literatur der Zeit*, Reinbek 1967.

BIBLIOGRAPHY

Merleau-Ponty, M., *Les aventures de la dialectique*, Paris 1955.

Mészáros, I., *La rivolta degli intellettuali in Ungheria*, Torino 1958.

"Sui problemi estetici del cinematografo" (A Correspondence with G. Lukács), *Cinema Nuovo*, 1958 (n. 135).

"Georges Lukács", in: *Les grands courants de la pensée mondiale contemporaine* Vol. VI., Milano 1964.

Mészáros, I. (ed.), *Aspects of History and Class Consciousness*, London 1971.

(Contributions by: T. Bottomore, D. Daiches, L. Goldmann, A. Hauser, E. J. Hobsbawm, I. Mészáros, R. Miliband, R. Schlesinger, A. Thorlby).

Mittenzwei, W., "Die Brecht-Lukács Debatte", *Sinn und Form*, 1967 (n. 1).

Morawski, S., "Mimesis: Lukács' Universal Principle", *Science and Society*, Winter 1968.

Münzer, Th., "Il giovane Lukács", *Ragionamenti*, 1957 (n. 9).

Neri, G. D., *Prassi e conoscienza*, Milano 1966.

Paci, E., *Funzione delle scienze e significato dell'uomo*, Milano 1963.

Parkinson, G. H. R. (ed.), *Georg Lukács, The Man, His Work and His Ideas*, London 1970.

(Contributions by: D. Craig, H. A. Hodges, A. G. Lehmann, I. Mészáros, S. Mitchell, G. H. R. Parkinson, R. Pascal).

Pascal, R., Introduction to *G. L., Studies in European Realism*, London 1950.

Perlini, T., *Utopia e prospettiva in G. Lukács*, Bari 1968.

"La riflessione estetica dell'ultimo Lukács", *Libri Nuovi Einaudi*, July 1971.

Pianciola, C., "Lukács in Italia", in: *Conversazioni con Lukács.*

196

Bari 1968.

Piccone, P., "Lukács' History and Class Consciousness, Half a Century Later", "The Problem of Consciousness", both in *Telos*, Fall 1969 & Spring 1970.

Posada, F., *Lukács, Brecht y la situación del realismo socialista*, Buenos Aires 1969.

Prestipino, G., *L'arte e la dialettica in Lukács e Della Volpe*, Messina-Firenze 1961.

Pross, H., "G. Lukács und der Realismus", *Deutsche Rundschau*, 1958 (n. 8).

Raabe, P. (ed.), *Expressionismus. Der Kampf um eine literarische Bewegung*, München 1965.

Raffa, P., "Brecht e Lukács", *Nuova Corrente*, 1961 (n. 22).

Raymond, J., "A Sharp Marxist Scrutiny", *The Sunday Times*, 18 Febr. 1962.

Read, H., "Georg Lukács", *New Statesman*, 2 Febr. 1957. (Also in: *The Tenth Muse*, London 1958).

Révai, J., "G. Lukács: Geschichte und Klassenbewusstsein", *Archiv für die Geschichte des Sozialismus und der Arbeiterbewegung*, 1925.
La littérature et la démocratie populaire: à propos de Georges Lukács, Paris 1951.

Rieser, M., "Lukács' Critique of German Philosophy", *The Journal of Philosophy*, 1958.

Rosenberg, H., "The Third Dimension of Georg Lukács", *Dissent*, Autumn 1964.

Rossi, P., *Lo storicismo tedesco contemporaneo*, Torino 1956.

Rudas, L., "Orthodoxer Marxismus?" *Arbeiterliteratur*, 1924 (n. 9).
"Die Klassenbewusstseinstheorie von Lukács", *Arbeiterliteratur*, 1924 (n. 10 & 12).
"On György Lukács' Activity" (in Hung.), *Társadalmi Szemle*, July 1949.

Runciman, W. G., *Social Science and Political Theory*, Cambridge 1963.

Rusconi, G. E., "La problematica del giovane Lukács", *Rivista*

di Filosofia Neoscolastica, 1966.
La teoria critica della società, Bologna 1968.

Salinari, C., "Lukács e il romanzo storico", *L'Unità,* 6 Sept.
 1965.
Saltini, V., "Ripensando l'estetica di Lukács", *L'Espresso,* 1967
 (n. 27).
Salvucci, P., "Lukács e l'interpretazione irrazionalistica di
 Schelling", *Saggi,* Urbino 1963.
Sánchez Vázquez, A., *Las ideas estéticas de Marx. Ensayos de
 estética marxista,* México 1965.
 Estética y marxismo I. II., México 1970.
Sander, H.-D., "Auf einsamen wie verlorenem Posten. G. L.:
 die zwielichtige Gestalt eines bedeutenden marxistischen
 Literaturhistorikers", *Die Welt,* 13 Apr. 1960.
Sartre, J.-P., "Le réformisme et les fétiches", *Les Temps
 Modernes,* Febr. 1956. *Critique de la raison dialectique,*
 Paris 1960.
Schaff, A., *Marxismus und das menschliche Individuum,* Wien
 1965. *Philosophy of Man,* New York 1968.
Semeraro, A., "Validità di 'Storia e conscienza di classe' ",
 Problemi del Socialismo, Oct. 1967.
Shneiderman, S. L., "A Visit with George Lukács", *The New
 York Times Book Review,* May 1965.
Sontag, S., "The Literary Criticism of Georg Lukács", *Against
 Interpretation,* New York 1966.
Spatola, A., " 'Inutilità' di Lukács", *Il Verri,* 1961 (n. 6).
Spender, S., "With Lukács in Budapest", *Encounter,* Dec. 1964.
Stark, W., *The Sociology of Knowledge,* London 1958.
Stedman Jones, G., "The Marxism of the Early Lukács: an
 Evaluation", *New Left Review,* Nov.-Dec. 1971.
Steiner, G., "Georg Lukács and His Devil's Pact", *The Kenyon
 Review,* Winter 1960.
 Preface to G. L.: *Realism in Our Time,* New York 1964.
 "Gifts of Terror", *New Statesman,* 30 Jan. 1970.
 "The Burden of Tradition" *The Sunday Times,* 28 Febr.
 1971.

BIBLIOGRAPHY

"Georg Lukács: a Tribute", *The Sunday Times*, 6 June 1971.

Stern, L., "Georg Lukács: An Intellectual Portrait", *Dissent*, Spring 1958.

Strada, V., "Dalla metafisica fichtiana di Lukács all'empiria deformante di Stalin", *Rinascita*, 1969 (n. 51).

Szigeti, J., "Lukács scheiterte an der Praxis des Klassenkampfes", *Die Presse der Sowjetunion*, 1958 (n. 113 & 115).

Terz, A., *On Socialist Realism*, New York 1960.

Teyssèdre, B., "Lukács et les fondements d'une esthétique marxiste", *Les Lettres Nouvelles*, 1961, (n. ʌ1).

Thalheim, H.-G., "Kritische Bemerkungen zu den Literaturauffassungen Georg Lukács' und Hans Mayers", *Weimarer Beiträge: Zeitschrift für deutsche Literaturgeschichte*, 1958.

Timpanaro, S., *Sul materialismo*, Pisa 1970.

Tökés, R. L., *Béla Kún and the Hungarian Soviet Republic*, London 1967.

Toynbee, Ph., "The Marxist Approach", *The Observer*, 25 Febr. 1962.

Ungvári, T., "The Lost Childhood: The Genesis of Lukács' Ideas of Literature", *Cambridge Review*, 28 Jan. 1972.

Uranga, E., *L'estética de Lukács*, México 1958.

Vacatello, M., *Lukács. Da 'Storia e coscienza di classe' al giudizio sulla cultura borghese*, Firenze 1968.

BIBLIOGRAPHY

Vacca, G., *Lukács o Korsch?*, Bari 1969.

Váli, F. A., *Rift and Revolt in Hungary*, Cambridge Mass. 1961.

Vasoli, C., "Lukács tra il 1923 e il 1967", *Il Ponte*, 1969.

Vecchi, G., On "G. L., Contributi alla storia dell'estetica", *Rivista di Estetica*, 1960.

Vivarelli, R., "A proposito di alcuni scritti di G. Lukács", *Il Ponte*, 1959.

Völker, K., "Brecht und Lukács. Analyse einer Meinυ ʒsverschiedenheit", *Kursbuch 7*, Sept. 1966.

Watnick, M., "Georg Lukács: an Intellectual Biography", *Soviet Survey*, 1958/59 (n. 23, 24, 25).

Weber, A., "Lukács: Zum Wesen und zur Methode der Kultursoziologie", *Archiv für Soziolwissenschaft und Sozialpolitik*, 1915.

Weber, Marianne, *Max Weber—Ein Lebensbild*, Heidelberg 1950.

Weber, Max, *Wissenschaft als Beruf*, München 1919.

Wedgwood, C. V., "History and Novelists", *The Daily Telegraph*, 13 Apr. 1962.

Williams, R., "From Scott to Tolstoy", *The Listener*, 8 March 1962.

"Socialism Active and Passive", *The Guardian*, 25 Febr. 1971.

Wright, I. (ed.), "Georg Lukács: a Memorial Symposium", *Cambridge Review*, 28 Jan. 1972.

Zitta, V., *Georg Lukács' Marxism: Alienation, Dialectics, Revolution*, The Hague 1964.

Zmegač, V., *Kunst und Wirklichkeit. Zur Literaturtheorie bei Brecht, Lukács und Broch*, Berlin-Zürich 1969.

INDEX

INDEX